"At the end of a very long day, when everyone was tired after four days of intensive training, German's charm, passion and enthusiasm woke them up, won them over, and elicited excellent ratings."
Drayton Bird—UK (The Chartered Institute of Marketing named Drayton Bird one of the 50 individuals who have shaped modern marketing, with others such as Tom Peters, Ted Levitt, and Philip Kotler)

"German really made us think and also motivated the audience to actually do something. There was no doubt at the end…we all understood that we needed to get what German recommended. Not just a great presenter, German is even a better salesman. Amazing."
Ales Lisac Slovania (Ales is an inspiring, highly entertaining teacher, having been named "Best Slovenian Speaker of the Year" and "Best Professor of the Year" twice.)

"The marketing seminar helped me to refocus our need to communicate with our customers. It was fantastic and we are reenergized! Now I am looking forward to taking on the world."
Peter Phillips, Owner—Phillips Plastics Ltd. UK

"I found this book extremely interesting and practical. It shows, in a very simple and functional way, the key factors of direct marketing, most importantly how to implement them effectively. It also helps to break certain taboos regarding direct marketing. Frankly, very good and a must-read if you are in this type of marketing world."
Francesca Maioli, Data Mining Manager—Unipost Global Postal Service, Spain

"German has brought a new level of Marketing Expertise to eDOC, helping us build a valued-based Marketing Strategy System for our customers."
Tom Meitzler, VP of Sales and Marketing—eDOC Communication, Chicago, United States

The Digital & Direct Marketing Goose

16 Tips and Real Examples That Will Help You Lay More Golden Eggs

By German Sacristan

Happy About

20660 Stevens Creek Blvd., Suite 210
Cupertino, CA 95014

Copyright © 2012 by German Sacristan

All rights reserved. No part of this book shall be reproduced, stored in a retrieval system, or transmitted by any means electronic, mechanical, photocopying, recording, or otherwise without written permission from the publisher.

Published by Happy About®
20660 Stevens Creek Blvd., Suite 210, Cupertino, CA 95014
http://happyabout.com

First Printing: September 2012
Paperback ISBN: 978-1-60005-230-9 (1-60005-230-4)
eBook ISBN: 978-1-60005-231-6 (1-60005-231-2)
Place of Publication: Silicon Valley, California, USA
Paperback Library of Congress Number: 2012948950

Trademarks

All terms mentioned in this book that are known to be trademarks or service marks have been appropriately capitalized. Neither Happy About®, nor any of its imprints, can attest to the accuracy of this information. Use of a term in this book should not be regarded as affecting the validity of any trademark or service mark.

Warning and Disclaimer

Every effort has been made to make this book as complete and as accurate as possible. The information provided is on an "as is" basis. The author(s), publisher, and their agents assume no responsibility for errors or omissions. Nor do they assume liability or responsibility to any person or entity with respect to any loss or damages arising from the use of information contained herein.

Dedication

I could never have written this book without the love and support of my family. I dedicate this book to my wife, Cindy, and my kids, Alexandra, Matthew, and Ander who are everything to me and give me their love and support unconditionally.

On the other hand, this book is not just about marketing or media technologies, but about people. I also want to recognize the people that have executed the fundamentals and basics of communication, and marketing and sales for thousands of years. This book is dedicated to those vocational sales people, regardless if they are dead or alive, for their huge contributions to the strategies of communication, marketing and sales, and for their uncompromised dedication to helping customers.

Last but not least, I want to dedicate this book to all the people that inspired me through the years. I couldn't have written this book without their influence.

Acknowledgments

Although I wrote this book, it would not have been possible without the efforts of many others that helped me put it all together. I would like to acknowledge and thank the following people: Brett Jordan, of X1 Limited in London, an amazing designer who created the cover; Dave Halpin who helped me clean up the content so others could read and edit it; Tara McMeekin for her hard work and professionalism while editing the content of this book so readers could understand and enjoy it; Dave Erlandson and Christine DeLooze from Caslon "the management company of PODi" for letting me share the real examples published in this book.

Thank you to Mitchell Levy and Janae Pierre of Happy About for publishing and making this book available to the market and to Jeff Hayzlett for introducing me to them. Thanks to Drayton Bird for his lifelong contributions to marketing—he is one of the best marketers I have ever known. Thank you to Charles Crouch for helping companies understand what online marketing is all about.

Special thanks to my dearest friends Joan Badia and Luis Virgos for constantly reminding me what a good salesperson looks like, and to my homeopath Eric Heugans from Belgium for inspiring me and teaching how to treat customers with care, unconditionally.

Thanks to Tim Lance from X1 for thinking outside the box and fighting so hard and smart for his business. I'd like to thank Chris Lyons for his interest in promoting my book, and Luis Medina for knowing how to get the best out of people.

A Message from Happy About®

Thank you for your purchase of this Happy About book. It is available online at: http://happyabout.com/digitalgoose.php or at other online and physical bookstores.

- Please contact us for quantity discounts at sales@happyabout.info
- If you want to be informed by email of upcoming Happy About® books, please email bookupdate@happyabout.info

Happy About is interested in you if you are an author who would like to submit a non-fiction book proposal or a corporation that would like to have a book written for you. Please contact us by email at editorial@happyabout.info or phone (1-408-257-3000).

Other Happy About books available include:

- #CONTENT MARKETING tweet Book01:
  http://happyabout.com/thinkaha/contentmarketingtweet01.php
- #GOOGLE+ for BUSINESS tweet Book01:
  http://happyabout.com/thinkaha/googleplusforbusinesstweet.php
- 42 Rules to Turn Prospects into Customers:
  http://www.happyabout.com/42rules/prospects2customers.php
- Red Fire Branding:
  http://www.happyabout.com/redfirebranding.php
- Social Media Success!:
  http://www.happyabout.com/social-media-success.php
- Competing for Global Dominance:
  http://www.happyabout.com/global-dominance.php
- Ignite!:
  http://www.happyabout.com/ignite.php
- 42 Rules of Marketing:
  http://www.happyabout.com/42rules/marketing.php
- 42 Rules of Product Management:
  http://happyabout.com/42rules/42rulesproductmanagement.php
- 42 Rules for Growing Enterprise Revenue:
  http://happyabout.com/42rules/growing-enterprise-revenue.php
- 42 Rules for Applying Google Analytics:
  http://happyabout.com/42rules/applying-google-analytics.php
- Collaboration 2.0:
  http://www.happyabout.com/collaboration2.0.php

Contents

Preface	Preface 1
Introduction	Introduction 5
Tip 1	**Understand the Value of Digital & Direct Marketing** **11**
	Example 1: Miami University United States 14
Tip 2	**Make Sure Digital & Direct Marketing Are for You** **17**
	Example 2: ScottishPower United Kingdom 21
Tip 3	**Recognize Digital & Direct Marketing Media Pros and Cons** **25**
	Example 3: Lexus United States 36
Tip 4	**Place The Media Where They Belong** **39**
	Example 4: Move.com 43
Tip 5	**Stick to the Basics** **47**
	Example 5: ING Australia 51
Tip 6	**Sales Productivity Is Not Just About Speed and Quantity of Contacts** **53**
	Example 6: Mercer Human Resource Consulting Worldwide 60
Tip 7	**Pay Attention to Marketing Shifts** **63**
	Example 7: MindZoo United States 66
Tip 8	**Preparation Will Help You Build A Better Strategy** **71**
	Example 8: Girl Scouts United States 83

Tip 9	Set Goals and Key Performance Indicators, and Use Resources Effectively 91
	Example 9: Kodak Spain 95
Tip 10	Proper Creation of Target Profiles Is Imperative to Be Successful............. 99
	Example 10: Citadel United States 112
Tip 11	You Need An Effective Data Collection Strategy to Win 113
	Example 11: Walt Disney Parks and Resorts United States 119
Tip 12	Successful Marketing Communication Engagement........................ 123
	Example 12: Fabory Germany 129
Tip 13	Don't Forget To Measure and Analyze Your Campaign 133
	Example 13: Arkansas Democrat-Gazette United States.................................. 137
Tip 14	Use the Right Ingredients.............. 141
	Example 14: One-to-One Mexico.............. 153
Tip 15	Beware of the Ten Reasons Campaigns Fail 157
	Example 15: Orthodontics United States 159
Tip 16	Become a Marketing God.............. 161
	Example 16: Chick-fil-A United States 163
Appendix A	Free-Bee Example: UNICEF Brazil and Final Thought! 167
Author	About the Author 171
Books	Other Happy About® Books.................. 173

Preface

Preface

When I set out to write this book I knew I wanted it to be simple, functional, easy to reference, and one that people could come back to as often as necessary. I want to share with readers a methodical process and the ingredients that will increase their chances of a better return on marketing investment (ROMI).

This book is about the fundamentals of marketing, sales, and communication that relate to personalization and how those fundamentals can be executed today with the help of a good methodology and the available digital technologies and media channels.

Most of the campaigns I see that fail today do so because the fundamentals aren't there. The proper methodology and ingredients shared in this book will help you execute those fundamentals today.

As a result of learning the basics of marketing and sales as a child, this is not an academic book, but a practical one.

I spent my school breaks helping my grandfather in his pen boutique in Madrid, and I remember watching with fascination as the salespeople, including my father, interacted with their customers. I saw them adapting their personalities and messages to who was in front of them. I saw them building information about their customers and using that information with sensitivity and respect. I saw how creative they could be to enhance the perceived value of the product that fit each customer. Even as a child, it all seemed very natural to want to help these people, and occasionally my father would let me. No one had to tell me what to do—I had learned plenty from the salespeople I'd observed.

Later on, my father opened a new business that struggled and eventually failed. He bought a silver and lead mine, and went from something that he knew how to do, to a completely foreign business that he knew nothing about. He moved from helping and building relationships through face-to-face interaction with customers, to dealing with large wholesalers purchasing his materials. It was a pure productivity-based business with huge investments in heavy machinery, and a lack of productivity eventually put him out of business.

At about that time, my mother had a friend with ties to an agency that produced TV commercials. She introduced my siblings and I and they soon began calling us for castings. This lasted a couple of years and my mother pulled the plug on it once my father's career was back on track because she was worried about us missing too much school. Still, it allowed us to chip in toward the household bills. It was hard work, too. Sometimes we'd spend an entire day shooting for a two-minute TV commercial. They said that everyone needs their 15 minutes of fame—I guess I was lucky enough to get more than that.

During that time, I was exposed to many conversations between the agency and customers about the basics of marketing and selling. They talked about the strengths of their products and the target audience that would be watching at that time, and they elaborated on how they could differentiate themselves from their competitors. They carefully explained to me what to say and how to say it in order to convince people to buy the product. I quickly understood that successful communication is not about what you say, but how you say it.

I quickly learned that no matter the product or business, the goal is the same: Marketing and selling are about successfully communicating to get what you want—something we all do from a very early age. I was lucky to gain all of this experience as early as I did within a real business environment. It's what made me the marketer I am today.

My experiences taught me the truth about business, marketing, and sales. I grew up with the solid foundation that successful business is, first and foremost, about helping customers. Successful businesses thrive because they do a better job of helping customers than their competition. I believe we need to look back at the business models of the past for lessons in exemplary, true customer service because it's something businesses did a better job of 20 to 50 years ago. In part, this is because businesses were more vocational—the butcher wanted to be nothing but a butcher and helped his customers with knowledge and passion. Money was not always the sole driving factor in starting a business in years past. Even employees such as waiters and shop workers seemed to be more sincere and happier in their jobs. Today, we see establishments full of salespeople and many do their job with minimal effort and don't appear to care about the customer. They do nothing above and beyond the minimum requirement. Or worse, they make a very insincere attempt at pretending to care, which, to me, is annoying and even insulting. There are also cases where salespeople pretend to care, and overdo it with scripted, sometimes creepy pitches that don't seem natural or make their target uncomfortable. For good salespeople, the ability to interact with customers is natural and never scripted.

The holistic and natural way of marketing and sales often get disrupted as we become greedy and obsessed with growth. I often travel to Mexico and the outstanding level of customer service in some specific vertical markets such as hotels and restaurants is due, in part, to a lack of greed. Their focus is on my needs and how they can help fulfill them rather than what's in my wallet. Ultimately, of course, they do care what's in my wallet, but they never make me feel that way, which in turn makes me a more loyal customer that will likely spend more money with them.

I am passionate about the core basics of marketing and selling because they have been ingrained in me since childhood. This book serves as a reminder of the fundamentals of successful marketing communication at a time when we seem to have forgotten them. In our current market situation, applying these basics is more important than ever before regardless of the media channels that you use to execute them.

Introduction

Introduction

"Marketing" is a powerful word, which in a way sells itself. Over the years we've given the marketing strategies fancy new names and acronyms, like "cross-selling" or "up-selling," etc., and with that, a perception has been born that we've invented a new strategy where success is guaranteed. But there is really very little that is fundamentally new when we talk about the principles of marketing communication and sales. I saw my father cross-sell and up-sell 40 years ago. The only difference was that he didn't have the need to come up with a name for what he was naturally doing. Customer Relationship Management (CRM) isn't new either. It existed years ago, but with only a handful of customers, marketers had no need for big software systems to manage the information, and no need for such terms.

The market has changed, but the basics and fundamentals of marketing have not. Marketers simply need new tools and technologies today to execute those basics in a very different marketplace. If you forget the basics, however, not even the best tools and technologies will help you get a positive Return on Marketing Investment (ROMI).

I believe marketing can be taught, but only the people that are passionate about it will be truly successful at it. When you learn it you can explain what it is, but it is when you feel it in your gut that you really understand it and do it well. Great marketers come in different ways, shapes and forms, but just because someone's business card has "marketing" in the title doesn't mean they know anything about marketing. I used to be naïve enough to believe that a bigger title meant more marketing knowledge. I quickly learned that isn't always true. Some of the best marketers I've met don't have a marketing title—and some don't even have a business card.

This book isn't just for marketers, but for anyone interested in communicating. It's about how we can communicate better to get what we want, whether it is to reach a sales goal or some other type of goal.

In marketing communication you never know all you need to know, and you can't generalize concepts and strategies. For every reason something will work, there is a reason why it will not work in a particular place or situation. There are no magic wands or crystal balls, but a good, methodical process will help tremendously in building the right strategy to increase the chances of success. There are a lot of marketers and messages out there that need to find a louder voice, and I hope this book helps them do that.

Communication is one of the most important things we do in life and promotion and sales come down to communication. We communicate to inform, but also to get what we want. The best communicators are often the most successful human beings (e.g., Jesus Christ, Gandhi). The basic fundamentals of marketing communication properly combined with the most relevant new media technologies can help you become more successful. We can't be successful communicators if we ignore the basics. In order to remember the basics and fundamentals of real communication, we have to think about how it all started.

Marketing communication started face-to-face many years ago. Salespeople targeted customers directly, one by one, in a personal way. This happened in two ways: customers came to them, or they had to go to visit their customers. This is called direct marketing. Direct marketing is the oldest and most natural form of marketing communication. This method is not the only approach to marketing communication, but can certainly be the most powerful one if done properly. It is so relevant that you can't afford not to do it today. In fact, most of the digital marketing technologies and tools available today relate to direct marketing. These technologies are here to help us effectively exercise the basics and fundamentals of marketing communication in a very different and challenging marketplace. Email, mobile, Internet (including social media) CRMs, and digital print are relevant examples of it. Because of their digital components, they allow marketers to create personalized promotional pieces for the different individuals and companies they are targeting. These media can all be used to directly and personally promote to customers and prospects. Be very careful not to ignore or forget the "old" direct mail—the postal service—because it is more relevant, powerful, and effective today than ever, as I will discuss later on.

Being great at direct marketing isn't easy. The biggest challenge is that it requires you to talk directly to individuals, address them by name, and therefore, you need to make sure you are relevant and helpful with your message. Recipients' expectations are much higher when they are personally targeted. If you don't address your target by name and you've said something completely irrelevant, your target will ignore you for the simple reason that they never felt that you were talking to them anyway. On the other hand, in the most natural world of communication, if you call your target by their name, it is because you know something about them and therefore they expect relevant and interesting information. Direct marketing is not about sending one identical, generic message to everyone based on your target's average demographic information and most common buying criteria.

Our current market, being so competitive and saturated, pushes us back to the basics of marketing and communication, which is about more and better personal interaction with our targets. It is interesting how we as individuals and the world at large go into cycles, always coming back to the basics. It happens with music, fashion, food, and even health—as the organic world is picking up strength, even a section of healthcare that provides old, holistic and natural ways of helping people still has its place.

But in the particular case of marketing communication going back to the basics is not as easy as it seems. Thanks to TV, radio and other mass media communication, we have been talking to millions of people in a matter of seconds. We can't go back entirely to face-to-face marketing through salespeople, as it will not be productive. This is where the new digital media technologies come in, allowing us to execute the fundamentals of marketing and communication, but with the productivity that we are used to. The challenge for some marketers is that they have never promoted or sold face-to-face in a personal way. So how are they going to do it from a mass communication marketing perspective? This book will help them do just that, although they will also have to practice to get good at it.

The stars of this book are not the media channels that transport our marketing messages to a target audience, but the marketing fundamentals and strategies that will lead us to succeed. I appreciate that digital media is a hot and relevant topic, and I will not ignore it in this book. It will be addressed in the right context, but only as part of the strategy, never as the strategy itself. This book will provide you with the methodical process and the ingredients to help you build a well thought-out, direct, and digital marketing campaign strategy that will increase your chances for more—and better—sales.

Tip 1

Understand the Value of Digital & Direct Marketing

What is Digital & Direct Marketing?

It is to retrieve and organize relevant information from your customers and prospects so you can use it to target them in a personal and very productive way, making it very easy for them to quickly buy from you.

Benefits:

1. You can quickly and easily retrieve relevant information from your target groups.
2. You can organize large amounts of relevant information in a functional way.
3. You can quickly interact with millions of potential customers in a very personal and productive way.
4. You can make it very easy for people to buy from you as your place of purchase in only a click away.
5. You can track and measure in great detail.

When doing direct marketing using digital channels you can also adapt your message, creativity, and communication channel to the person or company to which you're promoting your product. You can show your prospects the personal reasons why they should buy from you now.

Direct marketing allows customization—telling people what they want to hear—which is very effective in marketing. There are a few exceptions, where telling your target something they don't want to hear can be equally effective. In this case, you are highlighting the negative implications of choosing not to buy your product or service, for example, giving your target a scenario of being broken down on the highway without a service that will either fix their car or tow it to the nearest garage. In either case, different people usually want to hear different things, in different ways or places for the simple reason that people are different and buy for different reasons. That is why using the digital media, which allows you to change your message, creativity, and channel depending on who you are talking to, is critical to increase your chance of success.

There are always exceptions to the rule of individualization, however, when telling everyone the same thing is, in fact, customizing, because everyone wants to hear the same message. This happens with products in high demand being sold by companies with very strong unique selling points (USPs). For example, if you are selling the iPhone for 30% less than anyone else, you will not have to change your message to sell the product. You will tell everyone the same thing, which is that you know they want it and you have it much cheaper than anyone else. For this reason, it is always wise to build your campaign on strategy rather than on an application or a channel. People excited about personalization often think the more they personalize, the better, but this is not always the case. If you start with the strategy, you will know how much personalization is relevant. We will discuss this point in more detail later on in the book.

Direct marketing also helps you measure and analyze in great detail. Being personal not only allows you to measure how much you sold, but also who bought from you—and who didn't. You can measure who was interested, but did not buy and analyze why, and you can track your customers and prospects online like never before.

"To isolate your prospects and customers as individuals and build a continuing relationship with them—to their greater benefit and your greater profit."
—Drayton Bird, on the purpose of direct marketing from Commonsense Direct and Digital Marketing

Example 1: Miami University United States

Miami University had revamped its honors program to give students the opportunity to shape their studies and explore their interests beyond the traditional classroom. Their business objectives were to increase the number of prospective honors applicants and enrollment in the honors program.

They increased total prospective student visits by 32%, 300% increase in scholar Saturday visits, 45% increase of page views on honors website, 33% increase in first-time visitors to website. The enrolled an incoming class was 31% over goal. 98.5% of the suspects who were converted to prospects by the campaign came from the variable campaign.

The test portion of the campaign consisted of a variable brochure with a personalized URL. This brochure was sent to more than 20,000 qualified high school seniors. Follow-up emails were sent out several days after the mail drop with a link to the recipient's personalized URL.

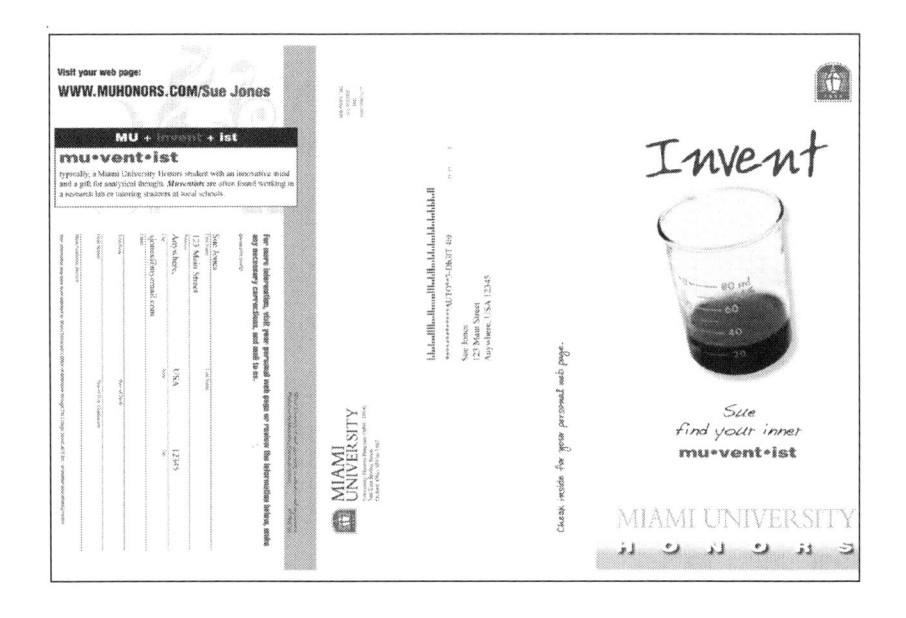

The Personalized URL was designed to convey more relevant information to interested students about the Miami honor's program and to capture more relevant information about the potential applicant through a survey. Students who completed the survey would then be contacted by honors peers whose interests most closely matched their own.

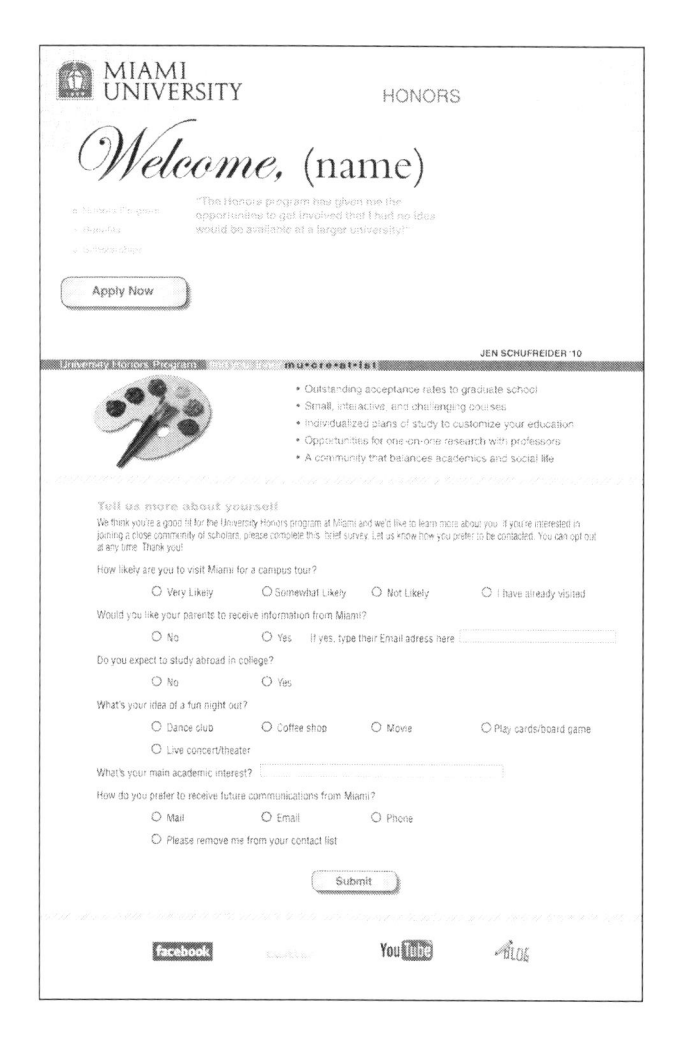

The Digital & Direct Marketing Goose

In phase two, 6,500 variable postcards were sent promoting the scholar Saturdays. Previous Miami research had determined that students who visited campus, especially during the highly regarded scholar Saturdays dedicated to the honors program, were much more likely to apply to Miami than students who had not visited the campus. A follow-up email was sent three days after the postcard drop. A second mailing was cancelled due to overwhelming response to the first postcard drop.

"Case study source: http://www.podi.org/casestudy, a collection of over 500 successful digital and direct marketing solutions in full color."

Tip 2
Make Sure Digital & Direct Marketing Are for You

Companies that successfully use digital and direct marketing share a set of characteristics that increase the chances for success. These characteristics include:

Feature-Rich Products

The company sells products that have many different versions/models, and it has a sufficient marketing budget for each product. This wide offering means that consumers will buy for many different reasons. Therefore, one is looking at very diverse buying criteria. These diverse buying criteria mean that you must send them targeted marketing messages that address their specific issues. Digital marketing lets you manage a wide range of marketing materials, each with its own message. Relevant industry examples: automotive, technology, education, retail, travel, real estate, entertainment, and healthcare.

Products with a Post-Sale Opportunity

These can be either add-on services or accessories that link to the purchased product. They offer a post-sale opportunity to promote selected accessories and services to customers who bought different products. This includes companies with a diverse set of related products. Digital marketing offers you the possibility to quickly change your message based on the initial purchase and post-purchase actions taken by your customers. Relevant industry examples: automotive, technology, education, retail, household goods, furniture, and travel.

Good Customer Relationship Management Systems (CRMs)

Companies collect information about their customers through many different channels, often placing this information in a CRM system. This information can help you improve the value of your existing customers to your company by knowing what and when they buy. It can be used to encourage customers to make repeat purchases from you. Digital marketing offers you the flexibility to pitch to your customers based on the information that you have in the CRM. Relevant industry examples: financial, insurance, healthcare, retail, and automotive.

Products with Weak Unique Selling Points (USPs)

If your product does not have strong USPs, it is difficult for customers to distinguish it from similar products. You might need to find your uniqueness outside of the product itself, for example, by maintaining better customer contact. Some companies are very successful in that; they communicate better with customers than their competitors, even though they offer similar products or services. The flexibility and speed of digital marketing will support a better communication strategy that can help customers distinguish you from your competition. The market is so competitive and saturated today that most companies fit in this category.

Complex Products

A complex product requires more interaction with prospective customers to explain and promote its value. This interaction can lead to better understanding of issues that need to be addressed to help customers make the decision to buy. Digital marketing allows flexibility to address customers in different ways in order to provide them with specific information they need to understand your product and see its unique value. Relevant industry examples: pharmaceuticals, healthcare, technical products, and specialty products.

Products that Need Longer Sales Cycles

As with complex products, products with long sales cycles require more touch points and longer relationships to be sold successfully. The digital marketing communication channels available today integrate very well, so you can send a consistent message to your prospects over time through multiple channels. They also provide you with the flexibility and speed that you need to improve your sales productivity during this long cycle. Relevant industry examples: specialty products and products that require a mid- to large-sized investment.

Transactional Communications

Transactional documents such as billing statements spend more time with your customers than any other form of marketing communication. Transactional documents are built with customer's information such as buying activities or usage in the case of utility statements. This transactional information provides great value to the company that deals with it. Digital printing is a great way to help you deliver the right promotional message to the right individual as a part of this communication channel. Relevant industry examples: utilities, telecommunications, financial, and insurance.

Market through Remote Channels

Companies that use distributors, dealers, sales representatives, and franchises need a more flexible, but consistent and integrated, direct marketing process that is effective, easy to track, and reliable. Web-to-Print (W2P) can help tremendously. You retain control of your strategy and your brand, but you allow your partner marketing and sales channels to help you send a more relevant pitch to your prospects. Relevant industry examples: manufacturing companies such as automotive.

Limited Storage Space

Companies that have limited storage space or need to reduce costs by reducing space can utilize digital marketing tools. On-demand digital production effectively provides you with unlimited space. You can store as many marketing products online as you want, then you can send selected items to your prospects as needed using the most appropriate method (email, print, etc). Relevant industry examples: Most companies in our marketplace fit into this category as companies are constantly trying to reduce costs and reducing real estate square footage is a major cost-cutting measure.

Products that Are Exposed to Constant Changes

If your company's products are constantly changing, you need to create and produce your marketing material to match this fast-paced environment. Digital production on demand allows you to make changes as needed, and then produce the materials to meet specific needs. Relevant industry examples: Most products in our marketplace fit into this category as companies need to constantly upgrade them in order to be competitive.

Non-profit Organizations

Non-profit is another huge category for digital and direct marketing because in order to retrieve contributions from people they have to be personal enough to convince their target that their contribution is for a good cause. Building relevant information from donors is critical to be successful. Digital technologies can help them do all this. In fact, non-profits are at the top of the list of companies using direct marketing to communicate with their targets.

Example 2: ScottishPower United Kingdom

This example shows how a high commodity business thrives thanks to an effective loyalty program using digital and direct media channels.

The UK's consumer energy supply sector is highly competitive and consumers can switch suppliers with ease: between 8 and 10 million do so each year. But attrition rates, especially during the first few months after gaining a new customer, are high. For ScottishPower, increasing customer retention was a strategic priority. Eclipse GB, a leader in the creation and deployment of highly individualized, data-driven cross-media marketing programs, developed an approach that delivered results that exceeded ScottishPowers's expectations:

- 81% drop in sales cancellations within the first 14 days of service
- 39% reduction in new customer attrition
- 20% uplift in customer satisfaction

The solution that Eclipse GB devised was a communications program that nurtured new customers during the critical six to eight week 'welcome cycle'. The program commenced with a personalized email message immediately after customer acquisition, followed by a digitally printed, fully personalized welcome pack, with both pieces linking to an interactive PURL. The personalized web pages contained relevant account information including application progress and important documents.

The landing page of the personalized website included a quick survey with two multiple-choice questions. Recipients were also incentivized with the offer of a prize draw for a year's free supply of energy if they completed a more detailed survey on another page on the site. Touch-points throughout the microsite were individually tracked.

The PURL allowed a level of engagement that customers had rarely experienced before via direct interaction with the ScottishPower brand.

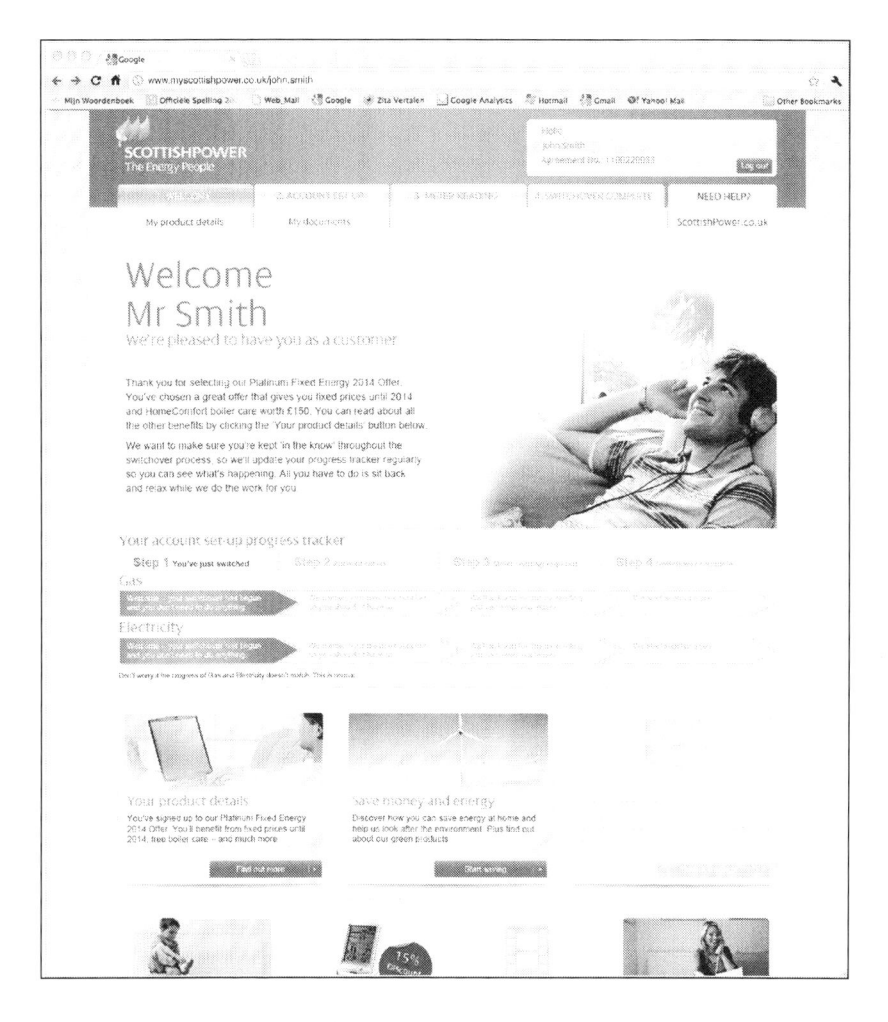

By providing a personalized welcome pack and linking that to an up-to-date, informative and interactive experience online the program helped to rapidly build enduring and positive relationships with new customers who otherwise had little loyalty to the ScottishPower brand.

"Case study source: http://www.podi.org/casestudy, a collection of over 500 successful digital and direct marketing solutions in full color."

Tip

3 Recognize Digital & Direct Marketing Media Pros and Cons

In order to be successful, marketers today need to interact better, more quickly, more often, and more cost effectively with their targets. That is why all new digital vehicles—including digital printing—with their flexibility and speed, are very relevant. These vehicles also complement each other and can effectively support your strategy.

These channels or vehicles will help make your next direct marketing campaign more successful. All of these channels are very powerful if used properly, but none of them guarantee success without a good strategy behind them. In order for you to choose the right communication channels for your next campaign, you will also need to understand each one of their strengths and weaknesses.

Email and Mobile

Digital channels have many strengths, but they also have weaknesses. For example, many companies routinely send out emails as a part of their marketing campaigns. But people receive hundreds of emails every day, so why should they open yours, especially if it is a generic message not designed specifically for them? People generally won't open your emails if they don't know who you are. The other day my daughter told me that I had 832 unread emails, and they were all marketing messages from people that I don't know. You are actually lucky if your message makes it to someone's inbox—most of the time it will end up filtered as spam.

Email and mobile marketing are ways to excel at promoting existing relationships. Once you start a relationship with a prospect, email becomes very powerful. It is more interactive, faster and cheaper to execute, and easier and cheaper to track. With email, you can add audio or visual attachments; you can also quickly direct a prospect to a relevant site by simply adding a link. But remember, if not tailored, prospects will quickly be turned off by your impersonal effort. The new capabilities of smartphones, including email and Internet access, offer a great channel to communicate with your target.

Mobile communication can be very powerful if used properly. Like email, it works better once you have a relationship with a prospect. Mobile marketing is very effective when used to quickly communicate something relevant, like telling your customer that a parcel will arrive for them tomorrow.

A few months ago I received an email in which the subject line read, "German Sacristan, Marketing Gold Medalist." I do not recommend using a target's first and last name when you personalize. If you were meeting face-to-face you would not say, "Hi, German Sacristan." You'd either say, "Hi, German," or "Hi, Mr. Sacristan." "Marketing Gold Medalist" doesn't do it for me either. You wouldn't say "Hey marketing gold medalist" if you were face-to-face, and what is a marketing gold medalist anyway? It really doesn't tell me anything interesting or helpful and it does not set the tone that there is something relevant or interesting in the email.

Postal Mail

Regular postal mail is seen as a non-digital channel till we add the flexibility of digital print to personalize and the interactivity of QR codes to send customers online. Postal mail may be most effective in certain scenarios—especially for initial contact with prospects. In this case, where you are marketing to people who are not acquainted with you and likely wouldn't open or even see your email, printing and sending by the regular post may be a better vehicle. People don't have two mailboxes in their homes, one for spam and the other for relevant mail. Postmen around the world do not scan and sort mail before delivery to eliminate the junkmail. Most importantly, people don't receive hundreds of letters in their regular mailboxes every day like they do in their email inboxes. As a marketer, that means you have less competition with a traditional mailbox than with an email inbox.

When people open postal mail, they are often more relaxed. They have often just arrived home and like to sit down and go through it slowly. Most importantly, everyone expects and accepts the fact that there will be some promotional material in their mailboxes. This doesn't mean people will welcome an irrelevant solicitation, or that they will act upon any recommendation that comes through the postal service. It is still up to you to effectively use imagination, creativity, and personalization to surprise and capture the attention of your recipients in a less competitive arena.

A home address also provides more relevant marketing information than an email address. The geographic location gives you demographic information about your target that can be used to increase the relevance of your communication. Also, people generally change their email address and phone number more often than they change homes. Therefore, a postal database is more reliable than an email or phone database.

With a postal message, you can also attach a promotional gift. With email, you are limited to one subject line to convince someone to open your mail; you can't add images and colors, so your creativity is limited to words. They say that an image is worth a thousand words, but when it comes email, the right word is often worth a thousand images. Using postal mail, you can add more creativity through images and colors in print. Recipients can touch and feel the mail, which offers a tactile sensation and a sense of quality. Postal mail is a direct one-to-one contact, the same as email and mobile, but on the Internet there are literally millions of marketers vying for people's attention.

It is also said that traditional print catalogues bring more customer loyalty than online versions. When your customers have your printed catalogue in their hands, your competition is far away. Online, your competition is closer, often only a click away. With postal mail, your message is usually seen by more than one person in the household, while email or mobile messages are only seen by the recipient.

It is clear the postal mail is still very relevant in today's marketing environment.

Internet

For store owners, the Internet is a global virtual shop where you can receive visitors from all over the world in a matter of seconds. It is also a place where customers are often offered free consultation services and interaction in real time. It is, without a doubt, a key place to be—the place where many consumers hang out these days. Online stores also benefit from unlimited shelf space while still allowing customers to easily find what they need or want. The cost of running an online store can be considerably less than having a physical shop in a good location.

The Internet helps us track and collect relevant information from visitors to our sites. Give visitors incentives to tell you who they are, and try to track their preferences and behaviors while they are visiting your site. The more relevant information that you have from your visitors, the easier it will be to sell them something.

You will need to drive visitors to your site. One method of doing so is to add an effective search engine optimization (SEO) strategy. There are some basic SEO principles that should be part of every website, yet many miss them:

- Write relevant, interesting content for your target audience. This is the #1 principle, and you will see why below.

- Put the content into good HTML structure, so both people and search engines can read it.

- Include descriptive meta tags on all key pages, in particular the title tag. Include a marketing message in your meta tags to encourage people to click on your search engine listing.

- Add proper tags on all graphics, photographs, videos etc., which describe them and what they contain.

- Use clean, simple navigation to show people and search engines what is on your site.
- Add a site map to help search engines navigate complicated sites.

The good news is that these are not difficult to do, and you can control the content. However, while these steps are important, they have only a limited effect on SEO. A good linking strategy is much more important for good SEO rankings. Links from relevant, trustworthy sites back to your site are essentially recommendations by others, and search engines note the sites that link to you. The more links to you from recognized high-quality websites, the more they increase your ranking as well.

Steps to build a linking strategy for your website include:

- Link to other relevant, interesting sites from your website. This is fairly easy to do and shows that your site provides interesting information for your visitors.

- Get links to your site from other relevant, authoritative external sites. This is much harder to do because you cannot make external sites link to you. They will link back to you only if you have content that they find interesting and valuable.

Many people will hire an expert to help them develop and implement an SEO strategy. While the basic on-site work is relatively straightforward, obtaining external links back to your site is where many SEO companies make promises that they cannot fulfill. They promise to get you a specified number of external links to your site but the quality of the links might not be very good.

Developing a linking program takes time and effort, but it also shows the best results. If you want to rank high, you need to work at getting good sites to link to you by having high-quality, relevant content.

There are other things you can do to publicize your website and encourage others to link back to it. Some ideas are:

- Start a blog on a relevant topic.
- Participate in other relevant blogs, forums, discussion groups, etc.

- Write and post articles, press releases and white papers.
- Participate in relevant social media.

Although having a good SEO strategy is extremely important, it may not be enough. Don't forget the benefits of some of the other channels mentioned earlier, such as postal mail or email to drive visitors to your place of purchase with relevant direct messages and QR codes or email links.

The bottom line is that it is imperative to have a good strategy to drive visitors to your website, but it is just as critical to create a website that makes it easy for your customers to find what they want and that also provides you with as much information as possible from your visitors.

*The office of tourism in Maine gathers information from their online visitors and follows up with a direct mail piece that includes information relevant to the visitor. This is a very smart combination of Internet and mail marketing.

*"Case study source: http://www.podi.org/casestudy, a collection of over 500 successful digital and direct marketing solutions in full color."

Social Media

Social media is relevant today for 3 reasons:
1. You can collect more information more quickly than ever before.
2. You can build more relationships more quickly than ever before.
3. You can interact with more people more quickly than ever before.

A good example of the power of social media can be seen in a video available at http://www.youtube.com/watch?v=yu4zMvE6FH4, uploaded by TheOnion on Sep 1, 2009, Facebook, Twitter Revolutionizing How Parents Stalk Their Children.

Social media is about building the right information that will help you be more relevant when communicating with your target. The right information can also help you launch the products and services that the market wants to buy. Social media is also about building the relationships that will generate the trust that makes customers want to buy from you, and it is about interacting and providing value to the different communities in which you participate.

Social media is not about selling products, but encouraging your target to buy from you. There is nothing really new about social media. Many years ago we went to social events to build information and relationships. Today, new technologies simply allow us to do so more often and with more people.

A good rule of thumb for a social media strategy is to ask yourself how you would interact with potential customers face-to-face and apply similar fundamentals.

Social media has become an important part of the marketing mix, and companies are investing in it heavily. As with the other channels mentioned above, you will need a proper strategy to be successful. It isn't about randomly advertising everywhere, but rather knowing where and how you need to advertise. The main challenges for a marketer are, as always, identifying one's target, capturing their attention, and telling them what they want to hear. The benefit of social media is that you can hang out in different places and observe. Listening to people sharing their thoughts is very powerful for obvious reasons. Knowing what your customers and prospects are thinking is priceless. It will help you identify the ones that you want to talk to and better target them with the amount of information that you have been gathering. You'll also quickly find out what the market wants and needs so you'll be more likely to bring the right products to the market.

When marketing via social media, it is all too easy to contact prospects too quickly, using the same media we use to retrieve their information. This makes what you know about your targets too obvious, and it makes it look like you are just looking for a quick sale. It is always effective to respond quickly and directly to the needs of your target audience, but it's the way that you do it that will make you succeed or fail. Sometimes it's appropriate to wait just a bit to provide relevant information and use other communication channels besides social media to do so. This will make it less obvious that you know what you know and make you seem less aggressive and more helpful.

Word of mouth has always been the strongest channel because you are using someone to promote and sell your products and services to someone they know better and have a better relationships with than you have. It even works well when they promote a product to a person they don't know because a prospect will likely trust another consumer more than they will trust you. Word of mouth works faster than ever before, thanks to social media and the Internet—but be careful because it can be both positive and negative and unsatisfied customers can spread their messages faster than ever before. A clear example happened a while ago when an airline damaged a customer's guitar. The customer made the claim and the airline ignored him completely. He created a very successful video on YouTube (http://www.youtube.com/watch?v=5YGc4zOqozo, uploaded by sonsofmaxwell on Jul 6, 2009, United Breaks Guitars) about his negative experience that received more than 12 million hits and he's planning a second and third video. It's possible that by the end of this ordeal the airline could end up getting some positive marketing, but as it stands now it's the negative message that's getting attention.

There are different social media strategies depending on whether you are on a B2B or B2C model. Consumers join a social network looking for discounts and coupons, while companies join to gather valuable information and build relationships.

Being the host of a social network will require a different strategy than being invited or joining one. Consistency is imperative. Once you start, you need to keep going, otherwise people will wonder what happened to you and your business. It is good to start slowly as you learn. Start walking before you run, but be consistent.

Newspapers and Magazines

Marketers can use geo-marketing when advertising on newspapers and magazines thanks to digital print. Publishers can build demographic information about the areas where their newspapers and magazines are being distributed and sold. Then marketers can adapt their offers and pitch to each one of those different demographics, which in turn will help increase the chances of more sales.

For publications that are being delivered to subscribers by postal mail, the recipient's name could be printed on the publication, and it could also be printed on the advertising page to help the advertiser better capture the reader's attention.

Unique numbers can be printed in an advertising page, and prizes can be offered to the person that brings a winning number to the advertiser's store or enters it on their website. This is an effective way to drive consumers to the advertiser's place of purchase. This strategy can also be used to build more information from the readers. In order for the reader to find out if they are the winner, they will have to enter a quick registration where we will build relevant data from that reader.

QR codes and personalized URLs (PURLs) can be linked to a particular demographic or segment and used beyond their ability to drive traffic to an advertiser's place of purchase. They can be used to measure how many people responded, how much product has been sold, who bought what, and who didn't buy at all.

Newspaper and magazine publishers are better equipped than ever to help advertisers sell their products and services. They can offer their customers a more personalized advertising product both on and offline.

Today, people also read newspapers and magazines on the Internet for free, thanks to advertising. But is Internet advertising really that effective? I am not so sure it is yet. Internet readers are very focused on what they are reading, often ignoring everything around it. If they do spot your banner, having a personal message attached can sometimes provoke more rejection. They will likely question what you know about them and how you know it. Just as with social media, you must be very discreet here. Again, a good salesperson possesses knowledge about their target audience without the target audience being aware of it. I am not saying Internet banners are useless—they do build branding—but they are not enough to convince a reader to buy from you now.

A better, complementary approach is to gather reader's information on the Internet and then use additional channels to communicate with them. As we discussed earlier, changing the channel can help make the marketer less obvious and also more effective. Publishers can require readers to subscribe for the first time in exchange for free content. They can collect demographic information that way, including contact information, which advertisers can use to target readers through other channels, such as the postal service and email. In addition to gathering demographic and contact information, this approach could also allow publishers to track the content readers are interested in via an online tracking strategy. This exercise can build reader profiles that can be used by advertisers to be more relevant in their marketing campaigns.

Even though this book is not about TV and radio, I'd like to quickly refer to these two traditional and powerful channels as they have also reinvented themselves. Thanks to the new digital technologies, they can also offer greater value to the advertisers. Now these channels allow the marketer to segment their offering and message depending on which area they are broadcasting in, increasing their relevance and therefore sales productivity.

Use Multiple Media

The value of individual media is great, but when multiple channels are used to complement one another it is even greater. For example, you can capture the attention of a prospect that does not know you by using a direct mailer. You can use a PURL or QR code on that direct mailer to send them online where you can track them and collect relevant information, which can then be used to follow up with a personalized email or direct mailer. By combining channels, you go from anonymous, generic communication to a message that is personalized and will likely increase your chances of building relationships and selling your products.

In a different scenario, you may have already collected a lot of relevant information from your prospects online and wish to follow up with a direct mailer or an email. QR codes can be printed on a direct mailer and scanned by a smartphone to easily and quickly drive prospects back online and drive specific desired actions.

Another example could be what I have been doing in this book. I have been taking you from a printed channel such as this book to a digital channel such as YouTube to show you videos that reinforce the ideas and tips I am presenting.

Example 3: Lexus United States

Lexus, wanted to create market awareness of the new Lexus 2010 RX sport utility vehicle and its customizable features. As part of its advertising strategy a six-issue custom magazine was developed, in cooperation with Time, Inc. and The Ace Group.

Lexus wanted to develop the branding message that the new Lexus 2010 RX is "Driver Inspired" and "Customizable." By experiencing the custom magazine and its personalized ads, subscribers would understand that the Lexus 2010 RX is as customizable as the magazine carrying its ads.

Lexus worked with its partners to develop the Mine magazine and test the viability of custom magazines as a viable advertising channel. To drive subscriptions for Mine, advertisements were run in nine Time, Inc. magazines including Food & Wine, Travel + Leisure, All You, InStyle and Money. The ads directed readers to a website where they could sign up. Subscriptions to either the print or digital versions of the magazine were open to anyone over 18 years old, residing in the United States. Subscribers were able to choose five out of eight Time, Inc. publications from which they would like to have articles included in their personal Mine magazine. While completing their registration, subscribers had to fill in their personal information and were asked to answer four quick questions that would be used to help personalize the Lexus RX ads.

In each issue of Mine there are four Lexus ads, a Table of Contents page and five 6-page segments for each of the magazines chosen by the subscriber for a total of 36 pages. The Lexus ads were personalized with the subscriber's name, home town, geographic region, state, radio preference, and more.

The Digital & Direct Marketing Goose

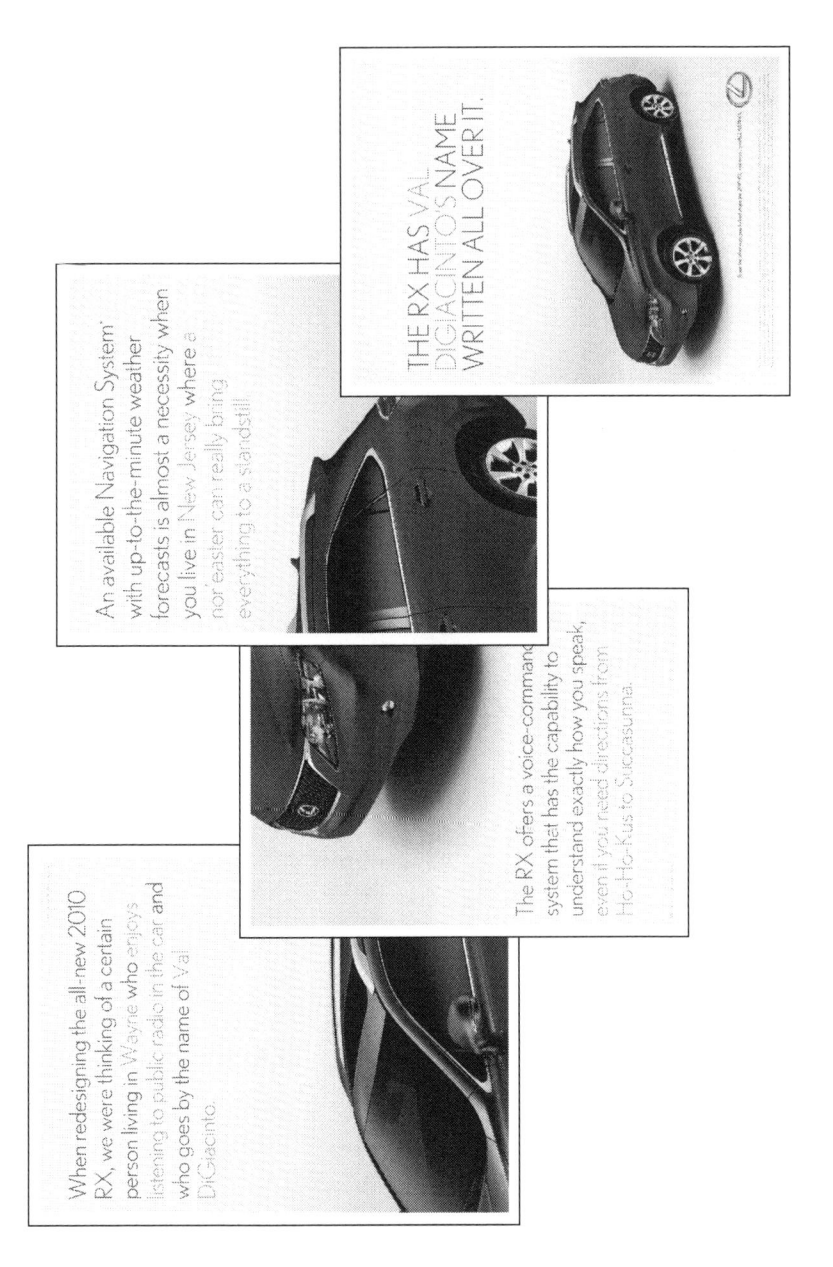

"Case study source: http://www.podi.org/casestudy, a collection of over 500 successful digital and direct marketing solutions in full color."

38   Tip 3: Recognize Digital & Direct Marketing Media Pros and Cons

Tip 4

Place The Media Where They Belong

The new digital technologies and media have not invented any new marketing concepts, but they have made existing ones more effective and productive. Marketing evolution started with face-to-face and one-to-one personal contact and has grown to one-to-many as technologies improved their reach and effectiveness. Not only do digital media reach many today, but these media can also reach them in a more personal way.

The media is the vehicle that you use to communicate with your target, but it and can never be the strategy itself. To get the biggest benefit, you must use media in the right context. Many new media channels have been launched into the marketplace very quickly. All of them are relevant and offer great value, but none of them alone can guarantee success—they must be part of a good marketing plan.

The market in general today—specifically some marketers and most media service providers—is obsessed with the new digital channels. Internet that includes social media, e-mail, mobile, and QR codes are among the most popular ones. Often marketers and media service providers invest a great deal of time and effort trying to determine the best channel to communicate. While all of these channels have a purpose, they each come with their own set of strengths and weaknesses. For every reason you give me why one channel is better than the other, I can give you a reason as to why the opposite is true.

You will not be able to be successful, if you only focus on the media and marketing technologies. I appreciate new technologies, but as with many other things in life, they have a negative side. In our quest to automate everything, we often forget to think for ourselves. Too often we rely on technology to do everything for us. In some cases this works, but not in marketing. While technologies help us execute the old concepts and basics of marketing communication in a very difficult, saturated, and competitive marketplace, they can't create an effective campaign without the ideas, creativity, and planning of an experience marketer and designer.

All technologies copy a person, making them more productive and efficient. Media and marketing related technologies alone cannot guarantee success because they lack the human element of the salesperson they're trying to replicate. There are two simple reasons why it is harder to copy a salesperson than someone such as bank teller, airport ticketing agent, or even a warehouse worker. The first is that salespeople are very unpredictable and can quickly shift gears based on what is happening in the sales process, and the second is that good salespeople are imaginative and have a sort of sixth sense, or intuition, that is impossible for technology to mimic.

Bank tellers, airport ticketing agents or warehouse workers are predictable in their work process, and in most cases don't require intuition to be successful. Their jobs follow a more mechanical process. Therefore, positive results are guaranteed as long as they follow the right process. Salespeople will increase their chances of success if they follow the right process, but they can't guarantee success because there are always factors that are out of their control. A forklift that copies a warehouse worker, an ATM that copies a bank teller, or an airport ticketing machine that copies an agent can guarantee success as long as the technology itself functions properly.

Conversely, in marketing, having the right technology is not enough—in order for you to increase your chances of success you will always need a good salesperson or marketer behind such technology.

New media aren't magic. Although new media tools are marketed as if it can sell your products by themselves, simply being on the Internet and having a social media presence and/or an email campaign doesn't guarantee you'll sell anything. People often tell me they want to do an email campaign without having any sort of strategy in mind. A strategy is key—choosing a communication channel before we know where we are going and what we will be carrying is like putting the cart before the horse. Using a technology or channel as the starting point of your strategy is fundamentally wrong and will only increase your chances of failure.

Marketers don't have magic powers either. Even the best marketers in the world can't guarantee what kind of response rate they'll get prior to launching a campaign, nor can they guarantee any numbers on closing rates. Yet, even though there aren't guarantees, a proper methodical process and the right ingredients will increase your chances of a better return on marketing investment (ROMI). Without the proper methodology that helps you build the right strategy, you're just relying on luck.

The strategy relates to what you need to say, to whom, when, and how you need to say it. The channel, together with creativity and sensitivity, is part of the how.

The creativity and sensitivity used in your marketing piece should also influence the channels you use. It's only when we ask ourselves those "who," "what," "when," and "how" questions that we'll be able to choose the right channels. You might need to use multiple channels within a single campaign if you have to say different things to the same person at different times.

Never choose the channels based on which seems the newest and most exciting, or the one that costs less. The lowest-cost channel may end up costing you the most in the long run if it's not right for your campaign.

For example, just recently someone told me he wanted to implement QR codes (also referred to as quick-response codes and 2D barcodes), but when we discussed his goals and challenges, it became apparent that QR codes weren't the best vehicle he could utilize. He had plenty of traffic to his website. The problem was that he wasn't closing enough visitors, and implementing QR codes wasn't likely to change that. The value of QR codes will be discussed in more detail later on in the book.

I see campaigns that I know will fail before they even launch—and it's not because I own a crystal ball, but because they're missing the strategy and, therefore, the basics and fundamentals of marketing communication and selling.

Example 4: Move.com

Move, Inc. is a leader in online real estate with 9.3 million monthly visitors to its online network of websites. Move, Inc. operates: Move.com®, a leading destination for information on new homes and rental listings. Move has local and national advertising relationships with more than 400,000 real estate professionals as well as consumer advertisers.

Move wanted to provide their affiliate agents with the ability to easily create and send highly personalized direct mail postcards to prospects within defined geographical neighborhoods. Move worked with QuantumDigital to build the Top Producer® Market Builder solution to meet the following goals:

- Create an automated lead generation program to build and manage agent prospecting in targeted areas.

- Drive prospects online and generate more listing business for real estate agents in defined geographical neighborhoods.

- Offer agents a variety of proven creative designs and personalized messages to drive traffic to web landing pages.

- Provide full automation for print fulfillment and order processing.

Many real estate agents rely on a process called 'farming' to build a presence within a new area and to find prospects (home buyers/sellers, listing opportunities). A majority of farming efforts include sending direct mail to targets within an area or specific neighborhood. The challenge in finding prospects via this method is that, often, the space is highly competitive—with more than one agent and brokerage trying to reach the same targets using that same method.

To distinguish an agent's direct mail postcards from the masses, Market Builder offers unique and personalized information printed on each card. Additionally, each postcard presents a unique passcode to the recipient. With the passcode, recipients can go online to a personalized landing page to access a free real estate market activity report for their area.

Each agent subscribing to the Market Builder service has approximately 30 postcards delivered each week to a portion of their selected list. During the course of the year, everyone on the agent's farming list will receive a postcard every four months. When a prospect visits their personalized landing page their name is removed from the farming list. To maintain the volume of the agent's mailings, additional names are automatically added to the mailing list from the agent's selected farming area.

Tip 4: Place The Media Where They Belong

With the personalized landing page, the agent is able to collect more information about the prospect, such as phone number and email address, to use for follow-up communications. An email is automatically sent to the agent when a prospect completes a visit to the personalized landing page.

"Case study source: *http://www.podi.org/casestudy*, a collection of over 500 successful digital and direct marketing solutions in full color."

Tip 5
Stick to the Basics

"Sell more stuff, to more people, more often, for more money, more efficiently."
—Sergio Zyman, on the definition of marketing success

Sales thrive when you can differentiate what you're selling and provide value to your customers. We all think our products are the best, and they just may be, but are they really that different from your competitor's?

Providing product value is easy. It's included by default; if products didn't provide value to enough people, they wouldn't have been developed in the first place. But product differentiation is much harder, and there are two main reasons why. First, products are defined by specs, which make them more vulnerable to copying from competitors and secondly, there are many companies in the marketplace today capable of doing so. Here are two relevant ways to differentiate your company from your competitors beyond the products that you sell:

1. Provide products as well as services to your customers. Vendors that can't guarantee a specific Return On Investment (ROI) on their products usually do this. Their

products require human expertise their customers don't have in order to deliver the promised ROI. A good example is a vendor like Kodak, which sells digital presses to printers. The products are great, but simply using them offers no guarantee that every marketing brochure or piece printed on them will be successful. So Kodak provides services—in the form of ideas, strategies, and actions—that go beyond the printing press to help their customers achieve the desired ROI and get the most out of the product. These companies fulfill their customer's needs beyond what is offered by the product itself. Vendors that sell products that require maintenance to perform at a satisfactory level also have the opportunity to sell such services to their customers. The major benefit is that a service organization is made up of people—and customer relationships are much more difficult to replicate than products.

2. Communicate better than your competitors. Effective marketing communication provides the best opportunity to differentiate your product and increase its perceived value. It's often the company that best communicates the value of its product rather than the one that has the best product that emerges as the winner in the marketplace. Communication isn't always easy and it's often taken for granted. Poor communication can kill you—quite literally. When I was little, my mom sent me to the local shop to buy some groceries and she specifically told me to only cross when the light is red. That is what I did and I almost got run over by a car. A traffic light in Madrid has two lights—one big one for vehicles and one smaller one for the pedestrians. The pedestrian light is lower and got my attention before the vehicle light, which was hanging high. The pedestrian light was red so I followed my mom's specific instructions and crossed the street. I was probably younger than ten and did not understand what red or green meant, I just followed what my mom had told me to do. Here is a link to a video on just how dangerous a bad communication can be: http://www.youtube.com/watch?v=yR0IWICH3rY, uploaded by grapjager on Sep 5, 2006, German Coast guard trainee

This book will discuss in more detail how you can communicate better than your competitors.

The basics of marketing have always been about helping customers. When you help customers you also build friendships. If your customer thinks of you as a friend, they are more likely to trust you and give you the information you need to sell to them. The customers that consider me a friend are the ones I've been the most helpful to and provided with the highest level of service.

You must determine how to help customers better than your competitors. It is not about helping because you have to, but because you want to. You have to be passionate about helping customers if you want to be a successful marketer. Some marketers are more focused on themselves than their customers. By focusing on helping customers, you are automatically taking care of yourself. If a potential customer doesn't feel like you honestly care about them and want to help them, they will never buy from you.

Effective marketing is about making customers want things that they need and value. By doing so, we create lifetime customers and constant positive word-of-mouth. Customers not only have to get excited about a product, but they also have to understand the personal value of what they bought from you so they'll use it properly. It's not just about a quick sale, but about making sure customers are happy and get a return on their investment so they will come back for more. More importantly, you want them to tell others about your product. Satisfied customers are your best sales force.

Marketing makes us want things that we then convince ourselves we need. Needing something is boring and rational, while wanting something is exciting and emotional. Needs and wants also influence buying criteria. The "wants" drive more diverse buying criteria since there are more reasons why we want something than why we need it. Ask yourself why you need a car and why you want it, and you will most likely come up with more reasons for wanting it than needing it. As buyers, we often need things for similar reasons, but want them for different ones. These are important things to keep in mind when you plan your campaign because highly diverse buying criteria will naturally push you to do more personalization.

It will be very helpful to know why your customers need your products and why they want them. The "want" is provoked by emotions. What will trigger the emotions that will make your customers want to buy from you? They'll be different depending on the individual so you can't tell everyone the same thing.

"**The aim of marketing is to know and understand the customer so well the product or service fits him and sells itself.**"
—Peter Drucker

A lot of things have changed for marketers but not the basics as it is shown in this B2B video.
http://www.youtube.com/watch?v=nXG7zYWKHGU, uploaded by BMAintheUSA on Jul 2, 2009, B-to-B Marketing Fundamentals Don't Change (Short)

Example 5: ING Australia

Here a good example of a simple campaign that brought a huge return on marketing investment for ING.

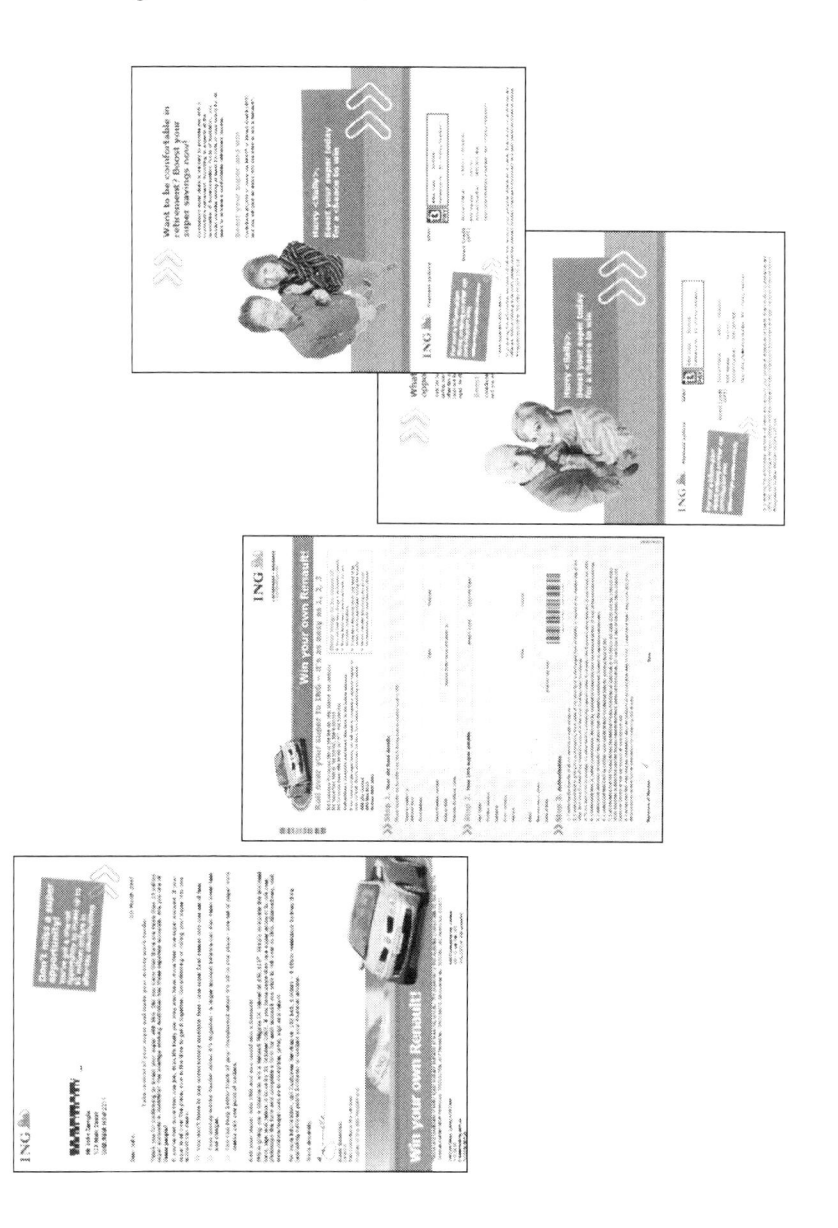

The Australian government made legislative changes to the way retirement savings were taxed, making it more attractive for ING customers to contribute to their funds. By using two simple but powerful variables—age and income—ING Australia was able to target messages and creative treatments to different profile groups to highlight the advantages of making extra contributions that specifically applied to them. As an additional incentive, an ongoing win-a-car sweepstakes was reinforced to maximize response. This is an example where simple customization worked incredibly well. ING raised an additional $22.5 million of funds under management resulting from a marketing investment of only $170,000.

"Case study source: http://www.podi.org/casestudy, a collection of over 500 successful digital and direct marketing solutions in full color."

Tip 6
Sales Productivity Is Not Just About Speed and Quantity of Contacts

Marketers are used to increasing sales productivity by focusing on speed and quantity of contacts. They believe the more people they can contact in the shortest period of time, the better. However, sales productivity is not only about speed and quantity of contacts, but quality, too. If you believe speed is enough watch this video. http://www.youtube.com/watch?v=0YGF5R9i53A, uploaded by RickBusciglio on Nov 2, 2010, Lucy candy 3

If the quality of your marketing campaign is not outstanding, it will be largely ignored. The quality of the campaign is not solely driven by creativity, manufacturing of the marketing pieces, or even the channel we use to communicate. It is driven by strategy and is a result of delivering the right message, to the right person, at the right time, and in the right way, as often as necessary.

If you ignore the quality factor, your sales productivity will actually decrease rather than increase. Being personal and direct through direct marketing increases the chances of saying the right thing, to the right person, at the right time, and in the right way.

Sales Productivity

Sales productivity is about increasing the number of visits or contacts in more territories, with more products, models, features, and services. The way you do this will determine your success or failure.

Let me first address the point of increasing the number of products and features. It is not just about launching more new products that will give more reasons for your customers to buy from you. As discussed earlier, you also need to address the fact that offering more products and features will make your customers' buying criteria more diverse. As a result, your promotional pieces must be adapted and personalized to address the different buying criteria.

Talking to more people in more territories has always been one of the biggest obsessions for marketers. You can do this in two different ways: direct and personal or generic and impersonal.

Direct and Personal Marketing

In direct marketing, the idea is to directly and personally engage customers and prospects to promote your products and services. Direct marketing is the oldest and most natural method of marketing communication. Although very effective, it was originally limited to a small number of calls over a specific period of time because it was executed by salespeople visiting people face-to-face.

The introduction of direct mail, which relies on the postal service to directly deliver promotional offers or suggestions to recipients, brought hope to marketers. Yes, believe it or not, direct mail as an application is linked to the most natural and effective way of communicating. The potential was huge, but it often fell short of delivering its promise. Although direct mail could deliver a fully personalized marketing message, most marketing campaigns simply added the recipients' name to a generic message thinking that would immediately make their message relevant and personal. Unfortunately, it does not work that

way; an irrelevant message after an attempt to personalize a promotional piece with someone's name will only cause a negative response from the recipient. The power of using a person's name to capture his or her attention was quickly spoiled due to the irrelevance of the message that followed. When we say something irrelevant to a prospect without calling them by their name, the negative impact is always less, as they don't feel as if we were talking to them anyway. Personalization isn't just about calling someone by name, but also about telling them what they want to hear. It isn't about randomly changing a message either, but instead making sure the chosen message is relevant. Simply changing a message doesn't work as you can see in this video.
http://www.youtube.com/watch?v=INOL2zVv7mw, uploaded by kickthecan2 on Oct 16, 2007, Katherine Tate Language Translator

As salespeople are at the source of direct marketing, they must be behind any given direct-marketing campaign. The problem is too often the marketers behind a strategy have never sold anything face-to-face themselves and, therefore, have not been in touch with the roots of direct marketing. Worse, some marketers will blame the failure of the strategy on the concept itself only because they don't yet understand what direct marketing is. They still believe that direct marketing is as simple as sending a solicitation letter with the name of the recipient on it. Direct marketing as described in this book is more than that and, again, its channels can be mobile, email, personalized printing, QR codes, PURLs, or any channel that you use to personally address a recipient. Direct marketing never fails as a result of the concept itself or the channels used to deliver the program, but most often because of a problem with the strategy.

We will talk about strategy throughout the book, but one of the biggest challenges with strategy is related to information. Sometimes we don't have enough of it, and other times we do not know how to use it. Information can either be built or bought, but often we feel that we do not have the time to build it or the budget to buy it. This is fundamentally wrong; in fact, it would indicate that a salesperson doesn't care what they need to know from their customers. Relevant information about your customers helps you be more relevant when communicating with them. Successful sales folks always have good information about their customers and know how to use it. When marketers fail to collect relevant information, their direct and digital programs are purely based on speculation and luck.

The positive side of new technologies is that they give us another chance to improve at direct marketing. They are great enablers that help us communicate in a quality way with millions of recipients. Most importantly, we need to become natural face-to-face salespeople to better utilize these technologies under the concept of direct marketing in order to increase sales productivity.

Generic and Impersonal Marketing

Generic and impersonal marketing was born as a result of salespeople being limited to the number of calls that they could make on any given day. This made business owners to complement this existing marketing and sales channels with generic and impersonal mass communication marketing in order to increase their productivity.

Generic and impersonal marketing existed prior to TV, radio, and newspapers. Many years ago, we were already talking to groups of consumers as they gathered at different places in a town. This mass communication meant generic messages based on customers' general buying patterns and average demographics. Initially, this worked so well that we quickly jumped at TV, radio, and newspapers as the means to contact even more people. This was a huge opportunity that allowed us to talk, not only to a few hundred people, but to thousands or even millions of people. As time passed, the market became saturated with advertising and consumers stopped listening to the messages. Advertising has become part of the background scenery, often going unnoticed or being ignored. Even when it is noticed, a generic message quickly loses credibility because it is the same as everyone else's. Take, for example, the use of the once-relevant word "partner." Everyone tells you they want to be your partner now, so it's no longer effective, or it is taken for granted for the simple reason that everyone is pitching the same.

We talked earlier in the book about differentiating our companies by the way we communicate with our target group. Tailoring the marketing message will increase your chances of being more relevant and differentiate you from your competition. Is it easier to differentiate when you can create different messages for different people or when you are limited to the same message for all? A message that is the same to all is much easier for competitors to copy and makes your message blend in with the crowd. Generic and impersonal marketing is still relevant to create brand awareness and influence consumers when they are in the market for a particular product, but it rarely drives consumers to take action in the way that direct marketing can.

When it comes to marketing, like many other areas in life, we need to go back to the basics—and this means one-to-one contacts. In this competitive, saturated marketplace, we need to improve the quality of our communication and marketing. A good way to do so is by going for personalized, one-to-one contacts.

Direct and Personal Marketing   Generic and Impersonal Marketing

Marketing In New Territories

I said at the beginning of this chapter that expanding to new territories will give you the chance to increase sales productivity, but doing so is not as easy as it seems. Years ago most businesses only had one shop in a single town. Now they may have hundreds or thousands of shops in different locations in an attempt to increase sales productivity. Here, the strategic marketing question is whether to use centralized or decentralized marketing across multiple locations. Centralized marketing is when the marketing strategy and the creation and distribution of the marketing pieces are 100% centralized in a given location. Decentralized marketing is when each marketing and sales channel creates and distributes their own marketing materials. If you choose centralized marketing, you will have control and can deliver a consistent brand message. However, you will miss out on the opportunity to allow your local sales and marketing resources, who are closest to the customer, to help you customize your message for each location. At the end of the day, these local channels are the ones that know your prospects and customers the best. If you choose decentralized marketing, you potentially put your marketing and branding in the hands of thousands of different shops and channels, where your key messages may become diluted and inconsistent. One technique to avoid this is to provide standardized marketing materials from a central point, which local channels can customize as needed. Web-to-Print (W2P) technology is a natural fit to help brand owners market more effectively across different territories. With W2P, you can create an online marketing portal for each location in the field to access. You will still build and own the marketing strategy via the portal, and you will decide which marketing products are the most relevant based on your strategy. In general, you provide direction and different marketing product recommendations based on different target groups. At the same time, you give your local sales and marketing channels the flexibility to choose what they need (also allowing them to modify some of the marketing products that you have online), when they need it, and how they use it.

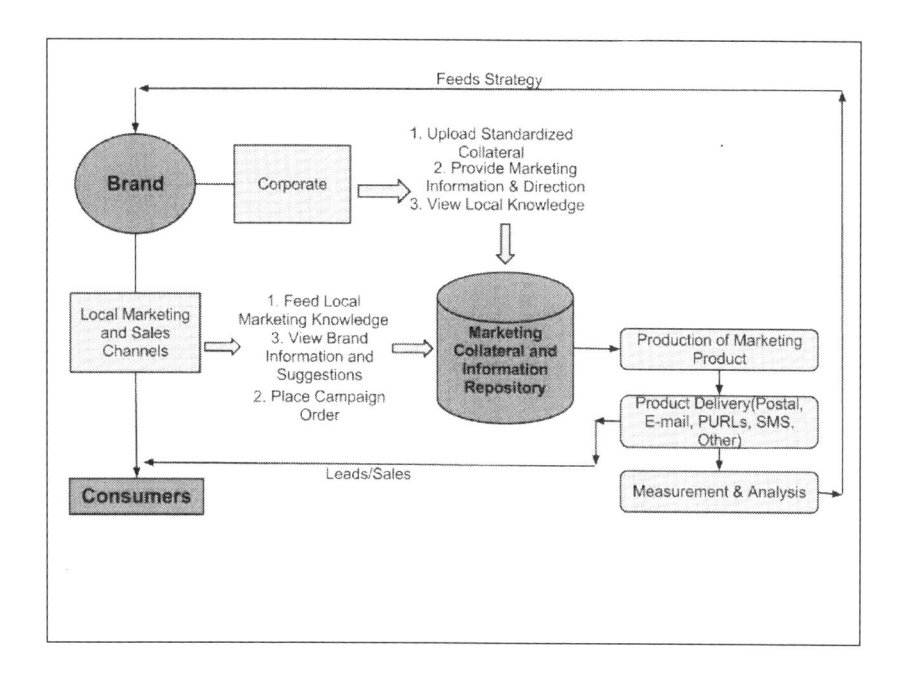

The figure above represents the strategy to get the best out of centralized and decentralized marketing. The brand will upload into a marketing repository or online marketing shop with all the marketing products available to its marketing and sales channels. This includes, not only brochures, flyers, cards, etc., but also promotional items, such as t-shirts, coffee mugs, or any other marketing material that might be relevant to help your channels promote your products. Local marketing and sales channels can access this marketing shop via a personal passcode. Different channels might have access to different marketing products based on what they sell and where they sell it. Channels can change and edit specific things from the marketing pieces that they have access to in order to improve relevance and effectiveness for the next campaign. Finally, channels can order what they want, which will be delivered in the amount of time agreed upon when the order was placed. The campaign can then be measured and analyzed for future improvement.

Example 6: Mercer Human Resource Consulting Worldwide

Mercer needed a collateral management solution that would reduce the costs and time involved in producing and distributing marketing collateral and support documents, simply the process of making changes and updates, allow easy customization for local needs while maintaining brand integrity, aggregate disparate materials into one, targeted, customized client leave-behind and enable fast, global distribution.

Working with Kinetic Corporation, Mercer built an online collateral management solution that delivers increased "speed of business" through cost-efficient, on-demand communications.

Mercer moved from a "Push" model of collateral management where the corporate office created materials and shipped them to consultants, whether they were needed or not, to a "Pull" model where consultants can customize materials and order only what they really need for their clients.

With the new solution Mercer is able to:

- Customize collateral materials from a Modular Content Library.

- Develop multilingual versions of materials that can be managed simultaneously.

- Personalize collateral materials with client information and logos, plus local office and consultant information.

- Create templates to maintain brand compliance.

- Institute true print-on-demand functionality through a regional print network (Americas, Europe & Asia).

- Implement e-Commerce accounting for each transaction.

- Implement a reduced 9-week cycle from design/translation to delivery—a significant multi-week time savings.

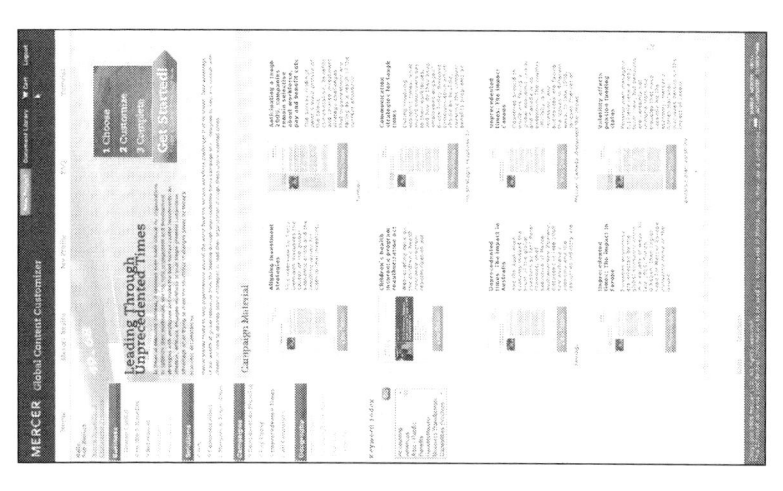

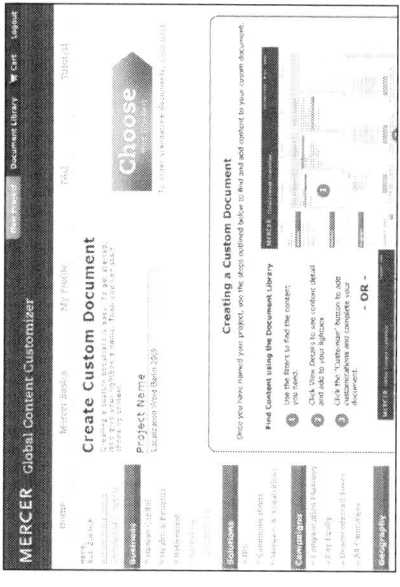

"Case study source: http://www.podi.org/casestudy, a collection of over 500 successful digital and direct marketing solutions in full color."

The Digital & Direct Marketing Goose　　　　　　　　　　　　　　　　　61

Tip 7
Pay Attention to Marketing Shifts

The primary change in marketing is that communicating successfully with your target audience is much more challenging today than it was in the past. The biggest challenge is maintaining focus and avoiding distraction by things that are irrelevant to the basics and fundamentals of marketing, communication, and selling. Particularly difficult, as mentioned earlier, is avoiding getting wrapped up in the excitement of new channels without first doing proper planning.

What has changed in marketing from past to present?

We went:

- From pushing generic information to customers, to pulling relevant information from them;

- From generic messages based on generic buying criteria and demographics, to personal messages targeting individualized buying criteria and demographics;

- From a few communication channels, to many different channels;

- From one promotional touch point, to multiple touch points;
- From pitching products, to interacting with customers;
- From the mindset that marketing is selling products, to the notion that it is fulfilling customer needs;
- From talking mostly about products, to talking mostly about interests;
- From quality products that nearly sold themselves, to decent products that require more effort to sell;
- From few necessary product changes and updates, to constant product changes and updates;
- From selling the same product to everyone, to selling many different products to many different individuals;
- From one place of purchase, to many;
- From consumers listening to most marketing messages, to consumers rarely listening.

Why did consumers listen to marketing messages more in the past? Not only the market was less saturated with marketing messages, but consumers had more time to listen, and media was new and interesting. As a kid, I remember watching not only movies and cartoons on TV, but every single commercial—and I enjoyed doing so. I listened to music on the radio, but I was also interested in and paid attention to the advertising. It was as if everything coming out from this new media was worth watching and listening to. That has changed today. Also, in the past, even if we were not interested in the TV commercials, we only had a small number of channels to choose from or switch to in order to avoid them when they came on. With all of the TV channels today, it is fairly easy for consumers to avoid and ignore most generic advertising.

In the past, printing and finishing quality made the marketer's job easier. High-quality brochures not only captured the attention of target audiences, but they also spent more time in their hands. Recipients felt bad throwing away a high-quality marketing printed piece as if it's quality almost implied relevance. Because recipients had more time to invest in those pretty brochures, they started flipping pages looking for something relevant and of interest whilst enjoying the quality of the marketing piece. They often took the time to look through the entire brochure and sometimes would see something in it that they wanted. Today we don't feel bad about throwing away even the prettiest brochure if is not speaking to us right from the beginning, and we won't invest time in something that doesn't show us relevance right away.

There were also fewer versions and product features in the past. Why do brand owners keep introducing more products with more features? Introducing more products and features into the marketplace gives customers more reasons to buy from you. This, in turn, increases sales productivity. This breadth allows customers to select the features that appeal the most to them, customizing the product to their own needs. Having a diverse product range, which can appeal to different customers with specific needs, allows you to better target your offerings and your corresponding marketing messages. The question to ask yourself now is: if your prospects will buy your products for many different reasons, why would you pitch them in the same manner?

After all these market shifts it is nearly impossible to provide value and differentiation today without talking about three factors: change, adaptation, and diversification. Companies that used to sell just a few products now sell many. Companies that used to sell products now sell services, too. Companies that used a few media channels to communicate now use many.

Being successful in the past was easier than it is today. My grandfather became a millionaire in the '60s just by transforming his tobacco shop into a pen boutique. He would have had a harder time doing that now. Today you just can't keep still, even when you are happy with your current situation. Keeping still is the same as going backward, because your competition is constantly moving forward. You always need to try to grow, and an effective direct and digital-marketing communication plan will help you do just that.

Example 7: MindZoo United States

Recipients received a personalized New Year's card that wished them a Happy New Year and directed them to a personalized URL.

> **Helping you reach a very specific consumer for a very specific reason.**
>
> Lifestyle Marketing
> Life-Event Marketing
> Event Marketing
> Partner Marketing
> Subscription Marketing
> Customer Relationship Marketing
>
> **MindZoo**
>
> 3 ½ South King Street, Third Floor • Leesburg, VA 20175
> 703.771.2490 • info@mindzoo.com • www.mindzoo.com

On the personalized URL landing page, they answered a short survey. The survey responses helped MindZoo segment the respondents into four areas of interest. Subsequent pages on the personalized website used messaging that targeted their stated area of interest. Shortly after their Website visit, they received a thank-you email from Jones that was generated automatically based on their visit and again spoke directly to their area of interest. The email invited them to call the company for more information about its services.

HAPPY ZOO YEAR, John!

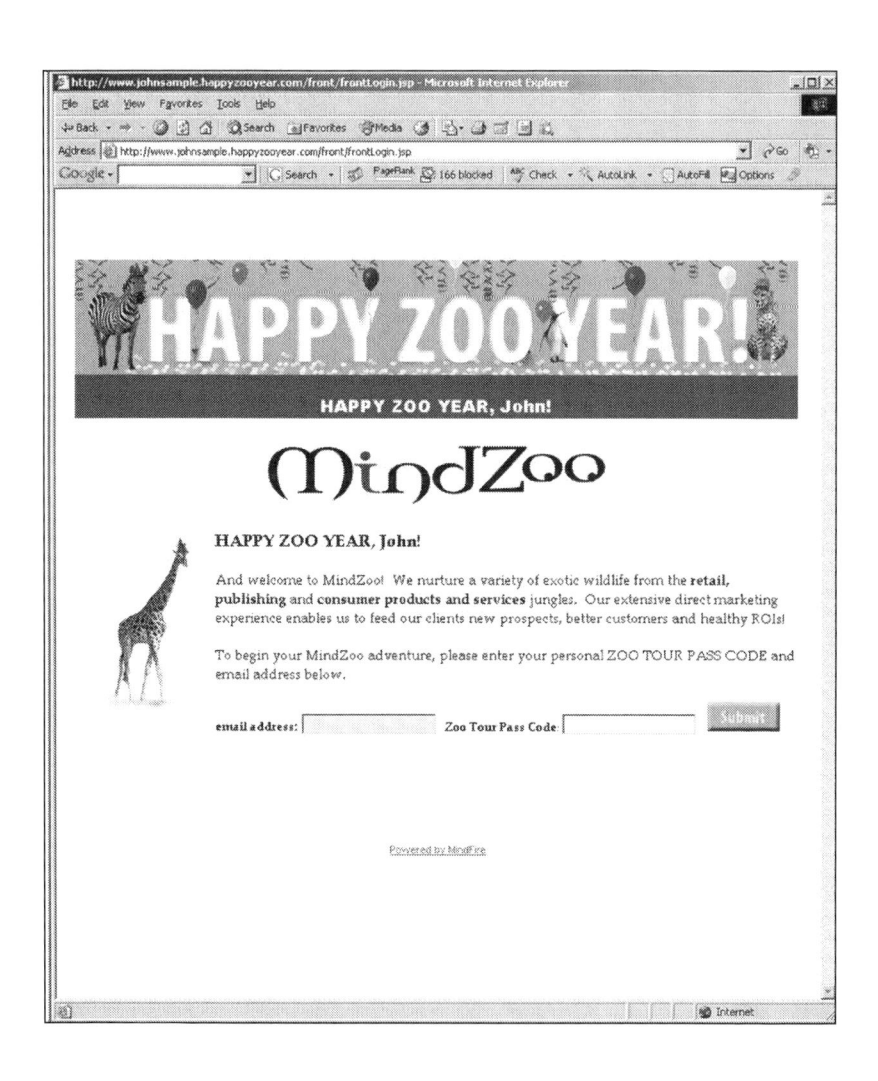

MindZoo

HAPPY ZOO YEAR, John!

And welcome to MindZoo! We nurture a variety of exotic wildlife from the **retail, publishing** and **consumer products and services** jungles. Our extensive direct marketing experience enables us to feed our clients new prospects, better customers and healthy ROIs!

To begin your MindZoo adventure, please enter your personal ZOO TOUR PASS CODE and email address below.

email address: [   ]   Zoo Tour Pass Code: [   ]   Submit

Powered by MindFire

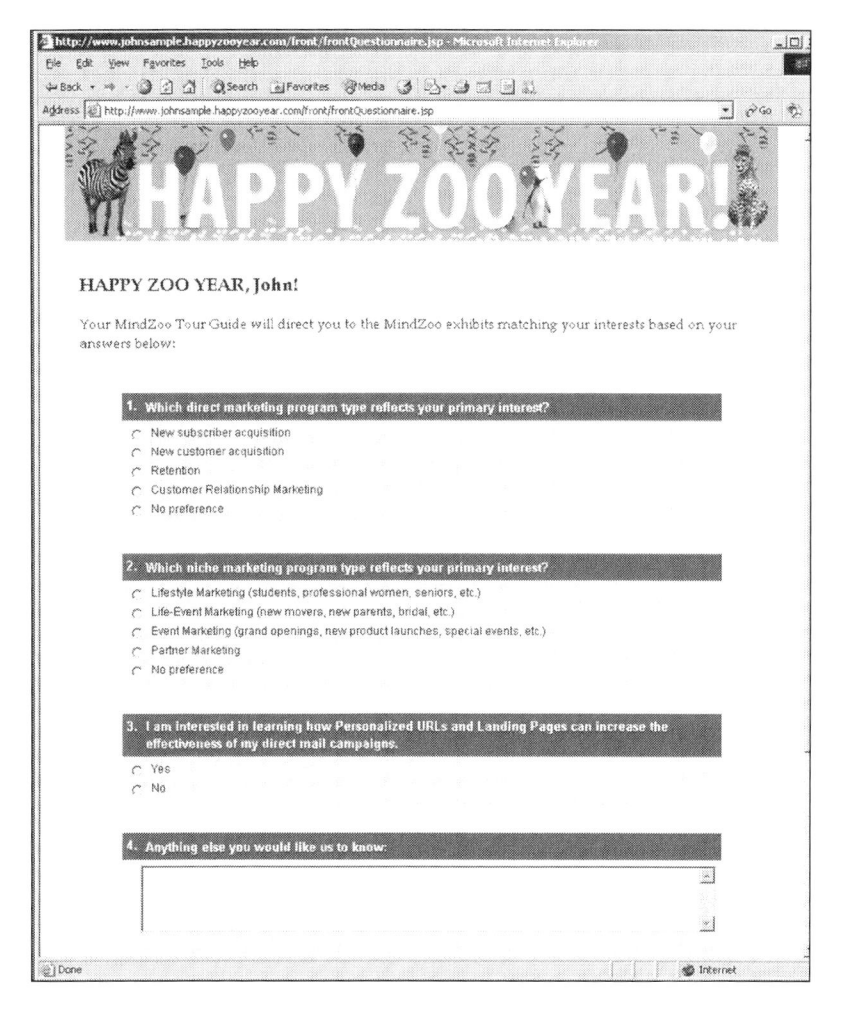

"Case study source: http://www.podi.org/casestudy, a collection of over 500 successful digital and direct marketing solutions in full color."

The Digital & Direct Marketing Goose

Tip 8
Preparation Will Help You Build A Better Strategy

You need to aim to deliver specific, targeted messages to the right audience at just the right time, and in the right way. Successful marketing programs always start with thoughtful and careful preparation and planning.

"A goal without a plan is just a wish."
—Antoine de Saint-Exupery

A successful strategy will be based on these five essential questions:

- What are you going to sell?
- Where will you sell it?
- When will you sell it?
- To whom will you sell?
- How will you sell it?

Defining what you are going to sell might seem obvious and easy, but it is not always so simple. It is one of the most critical parts of your strategy. I met the owner of a great company in the United Kingdom called Phillips Plastics. His company produces a wide range of plastic products that relate to marketing, from simple binders, pen and business card holders and bags, to customized products. It's an extremely creative company that can realize any vision of a marketing piece in plastic. I asked him, "What do you sell?" He answered, "Plastic products," but when he showed me the products I saw very creative promotional packaging, as well as other unique promotional items. The company was selling itself and its marketing vision short by defining what it sold simply as "plastic products." They could have better defined themselves as a business that creates marketing ideas that help companies thrive.

Whenever I consult with someone, the first thing I do is ask them what they sell. If you don't properly define that right from the beginning, you will likely fall short in creating a successful marketing strategy. After defining what you sell, you must turn your attention to identifying where and to whom you'll sell. Only then you will be ready to choose when and how to sell.

In order to build the right marketing strategy you must first analyze your product and brand, then your market, including your target audience, competitors and economic climate. Last, but not least, you must analyze your history, including all of your past marketing activities.

Product and Brand Evaluation

This diagram shows seven different facets involved in evaluating your product or service and brand offering.

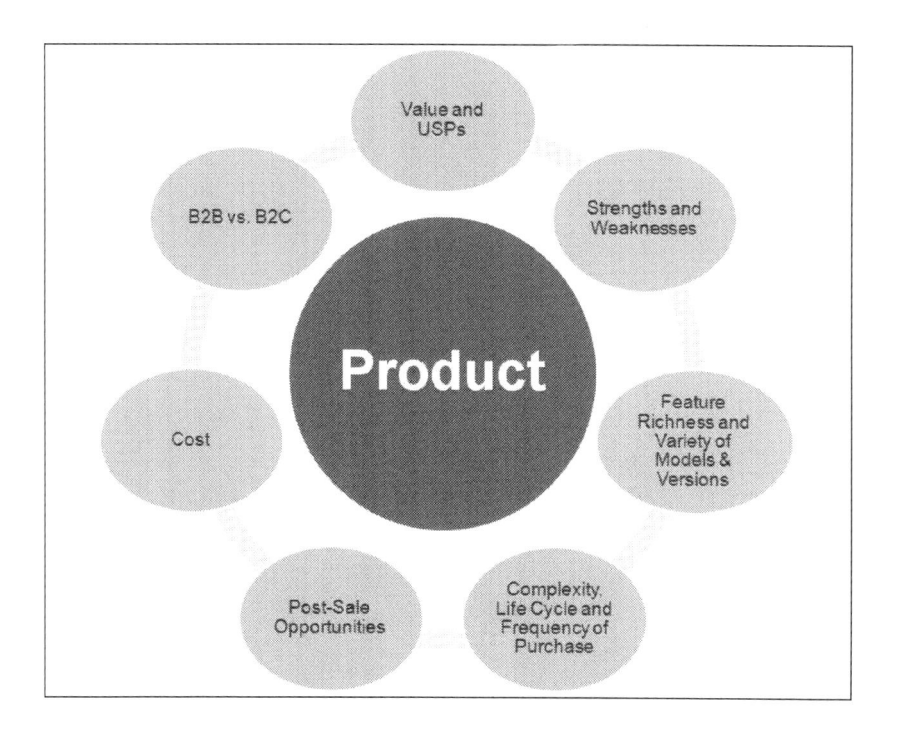

Diagram: **Product** (center) surrounded by: Value and USPs; Strengths and Weaknesses; Feature Richness and Variety of Models & Versions; Complexity, Life Cycle and Frequency of Purchase; Post-Sale Opportunities; Cost; B2B vs. B2C.

Value and USPs

What value are you offering your customers? What is your unique selling point? You should profile and identify your targets based on your USP, not just your product or service. Your USPs relate not only to you products and services, but also to your brand. Making the market aware of and interested in your products and/or services is not enough. You need to drive prospects to you and away from your competitors by showing why your USPs fit better with their specific needs. If you do not have a strong USP, you will need to differentiate yourself through the way that you communicate the value of your product and brand.

In addition, if you don't have a strong USP and are in a commodity business with very little differentiation, you need to close your prospects very quickly. Otherwise, they are more likely to check out your competitors who offer a similar value. Ask yourself: How can I make it very easy for my prospects to buy from me immediately? Then put your answer into action.

Strengths and Weaknesses

Identifying a brand and its product's strengths is always important, as they are often prospective USPs. Identifying the weaknesses in your product is equally important, as it gives you an opportunity to fix them. Recognizing both will also be critical in better identifying your target audience and improving your offer.

Feature Richness and Variety of Versions

Feature-rich products, or products that have many different versions/models, will have extremely diverse buying criteria. This means you must deliver different marketing messages for different individuals.

Complexity, Life Cycle, and Frequency of Purchase

Complex products normally need more interaction with prospective customers and, therefore, more contact points. Working across different media channels can be very effective here.

High-frequency purchase products normally have large target audiences with short sale cycles. They are often low-cost products and will not have much marketing budget per product. Therefore, you must constantly deliver a low-cost marketing message to a large, diverse audience. High-speed inkjet technology and other low-cost digital channels such as email and mobile will be very useful in preparing and sending these messages.

Post-Sale Opportunities

To capitalize on post-sale opportunities you need to be very close to your customers right after the sale. Timing is critical here, as there is a narrow window of opportunity for further sales. Servicing post-sale opportunities means delivering the right offer at the right time to the right customer.

B2B vs. B2C

Products or services that function as a business-to-business model, or B2B, can be different from the business-to-consumer model, or B2C, in many ways.

- Buyers often act differently when they buy for themselves vs. their companies. When you buy for yourself you might be more driven by the want or desire that we previously talked about. When you buy for your company, you are more likely to be focused on the need than the want, so your purchase might be more rational.

- Today, databases in general are more unreliable in the B2B model than the B2C model because people leave jobs or are laid off more frequently than they change homes.

- B2B sales are normally larger, but with a lower frequency than B2C sales. They target smaller groups, often involve more service offerings, and require more contacts to close a sale.

- B2B often has more knowledgeable target customer groups than B2C, and therefore, more and better information may be needed to sell to this group.

- Often longer sales cycles and relationships are needed in the B2B model, requiring a larger marketing outlay per potential buyer.

- Normally a salesperson will close the deal in a B2B model vs. the customer directly buying the product from the place of purchase in the B2C model.

- Points of purchases will also be different in both models.

- The models use social media differently. B2C customers use social media to get discounts and coupons, while B2B customers use it to build knowledge and relationships.

- B2C customers are often more loyal to a brand than B2B customers, who also tend to be more price sensitive.

After you have finished analyzing your product or service's strengths and weaknesses, it is imperative to do the same thing with your brand.

Knowing Your Market

Knowing the market you intend to sell to is critical for success. A good market analysis will show overall market conditions, the best way for your business to approach this market, and how your competitors will react. All of these are needed in order to plan for a successful marketing campaign.

Diagram: "Market" at center, surrounded by: Target Market, Awareness, Perception, Share, Economic Climate, Competition, Partners, Other Opportunities and Threats.

Target Market

How do you identify your target groups in the marketplace? Look at your product and brand strengths and weaknesses, your current market opportunities and threats, and your own sales history for guidance.

Market Awareness

Is the market aware of your product and brand? If so, you have less explaining to do. Campaigns could fail for this reason. If your target is aware of your product and you are treating them like they are not, you are overwhelming them with information they already have. If, on the other hand, you are treating your target as if they know more about your product and brand that they really do, you will not provide enough useful information to make them buy from you.

Perception

You will need to convince customers that you can help them more than your competitors. This often goes beyond the product itself, so don't be too product focused.

Perception of your company and product to potential customers is the most important factor in marketing and selling, so find out how the market perceives your company and product—don't guess! If you have a perception issue, you need to address it before anything else. Use your happy customers as a resource to help you understand what you need to improve and most importantly, use them to help you change that perception. If your brand has a poor perception in the marketplace, no one will believe it is wonderful no matter how much you tell them that it is. Using satisfied customers to tell the story for you is more effective because the market is more likely to believe other customers. The hardest thing to recognize and accept is that we sometimes perceive our brands and products to be better than they actually are. When it comes to perception in business, we can't afford to lie to ourselves. If you are unaware of potential customers' perception of your company and product in the marketplace, if you want to turn a blind eye to it, or if you have an incorrect understanding of it, you're putting your business at risk. Market perception is reality and can either kill you or help you to thrive. Time and time again, companies waste millions of dollars promoting the wrong way simply because market perception isn't part of their plan.

As Al Ries and Jack Trout have said, "Marketing is not a battle of products; it's a battle of perceptions."

Analyzing Market and Sales Numbers

Comparing your market share and closing rates is a critical exercise. If your market share is low, but your closing rate is high, you have to do more awareness programs. If your market share and closing rates are both high, you are in good shape; keep doing what you're doing. If your market share and closing rates are both low, you need to identify whether the problems are at the demand generation or closing stage, and then fix them.

Climate, Competition, Partners, Other Opportunities and Threats

It is imperative to look at your market opportunities and threats, including partners, competition, and economic climate.

Your partners and competitors will influence your USPs. The overall economic climate will affect your target groups. You need to look at your data and identify which customers will still buy under economic pressure. Why waste resources on individuals that will never buy from you today?

Other opportunities and threats may also be present, or may appear at any time. Be on the lookout for them, and be ready to address them as they occur. Market opportunities and threats together with products and brands' strengths and weaknesses are critical to a good SWOT analysis that will not only help you identify your target, but also help you figure out what you have to say to them and how to say it.

History

The old saying, "Those who fail to learn from history are doomed to repeat it," holds true in marketing. Companies repeat the same failed marketing campaigns over and over because they did not critically examine their own history. Looking at your history also helps you identify what works so you can invest more in what has proven to be successful while fixing what hasn't been successful.

You must know what you have done before, what worked, what did not work, and most importantly, why.

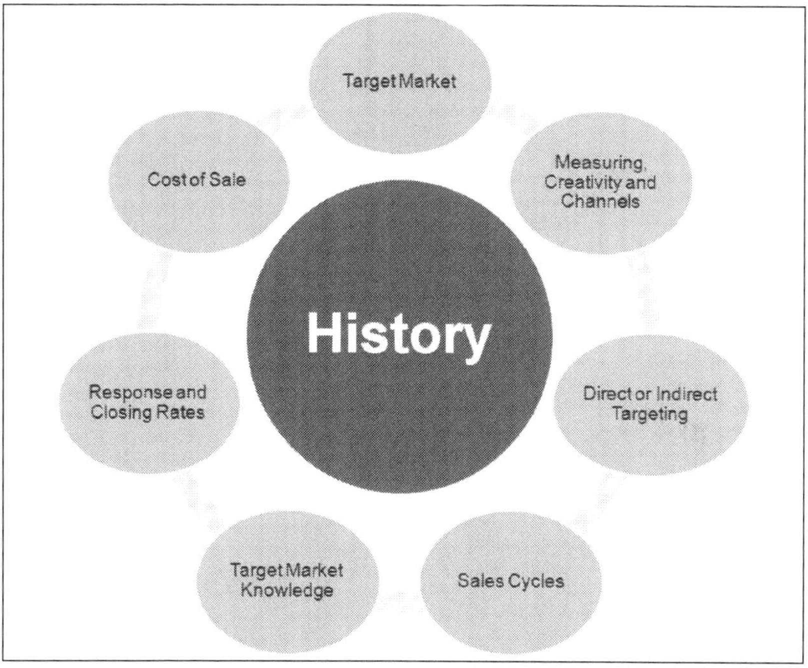
Target Market
Measuring, Creativity and Channels
Direct or Indirect Targeting
Sales Cycles
Target Market Knowledge
Response and Closing Rates
Cost of Sale
History

Target Market

Who were your principal target groups? Who responded to your marketing campaigns and who didn't, who bought what, and why did they buy? Who did not buy and why?

Messaging, Creativity, and Channels

What message did you send? Did it accurately reflect your offering and appeal to your target group?

How creative was your message? Did it stand out from others, and did it portray you as a unique company?

What channels did you use to send your marketing messages?

Targeting

Did you target consumers directly? Or did you use others to sell the product for you? If you used others, how did they help you? How can they be an active part of your strategy? I saw a great example of this at a grocery store when I was living in Belgium. Carrefour targeted my kids, advertising a free toy after I spent a certain amount of money. This was very smart, as my kids have information and direct access to me 24 hours a day. On top of that, my kids are the most persistent salespeople that I've seen. They never give up!

Sales Cycles

What are the average sales cycles of your product? Can you improve them in terms of time or number of steps? A shorter sales cycle will influence the number of initial contacts that you need to make a sale.

Target Market Knowledge

What do you know about your target group, and is what you know enough to make them buy from you? How are you going to find out what you don't know about your target group? Can you use what you already know to find out what you don't know? How will you use what you know to make consumers buy from you?

Response and Closing Rates

Comparing response rates and closing rates is another helpful exercise. Do you have enough responses, but fail to close sales, or do you lack enough responses to close a sale? Based on these answers, your strategy should be different. If you don't have enough responses, it could be because you haven't done enough marketing activity or what you have done is wrong. Maybe you are talking to the wrong people or saying the wrong things, or perhaps you have a perception issue that you have not yet recognized. If, on the other hand, you have responses, but not enough closings, you first need to analyze the person closing the deals for your company and what is wrong there. If potential buyers are going to your place of purchase to buy your products, you need to analyze what is not working there. Is it easy to buy from you? Historically marketers thought that the higher the response, the bigger the sales. Although this could hold true today, things have changed dramatically. In the past, there was less competition and customers had more patience to hang in there with you. Today, the competition is brutal and only a click away on the Internet. If there isn't a healthy balance between response and closing rates, you need to fix what is broken. When the responses do not work it is obvious that we need to fix that before we carry on. On the other hand, when it is the closing that doesn't seem to be working, we often carry on investing more money and effort to increase the volume of responses in hopes that this will make up for the bad closing results. It is important to balance our efforts. If there is a problem with closing, we need to fix it before we invest more money to drive more people to our place of purchase. This is very dangerous because a good promotion with an unsuccessful closing may only be driving customers to your competitors.

Cost of Sale

How much is it costing you to close a sale? How much marketing money are you investing per prospect or customer? How can you reduce the cost of closing a sale? If you don't invest the right amount of marketing money per customer or prospect, you will not stand a chance. The estimated cost of a sale should influence how you invest your marketing budget.

Always question your existing marketing activities:

You should ask yourself again and again about the objectives of any ongoing marketing activity. By doing so, you make sure you are utilizing the best strategy and resources available at any given time. Ten years ago I was with the director of marketing of a financial company in Europe. We were talking about their different marketing activities when a brochure that was on his desk caught my intention. I asked him about the goal and objectives of that brochure and he told me that it was used to promote different financial funds. He said that the two main objectives were to inform existing customers of their funds while trying to cross and up-sell them to other relevant ones. I asked him about how many of their customers had more than one fund and his answer was only 5% or so. The brochure was 45 pages long and each page described one fund. We started to talk about how little time customers had those days. We challenged the strategy and thought that as the majority of their customers had only one fund, most likely they were not going to invest too much time trying to find it in a 45 page brochure while reading the other 44 to see which one was more relevant to them. Then we thought about how digital print could help. By using this technology, they could have a better chance of achieving their two objectives. First to better capture the attention of each customer with a personalized cover that stresses the fact that this brochure has been done just for them. On the first page we can show the fund that each customer has which directly links to the first objective of informing each customer of their existing funds. Now that the customer no longer perceives the brochure as a marketing piece, we will make 2 to 3 recommendations on the following pages that fit that particular profile. A new technology or resource can change your strategy giving you the opportunity to improve your sales productivity. Just keep close to the objectives of each ongoing marketing activity and to the new technologies and resources available at any given time.

Go2Market

Do you have a direct or indirect marketing/sales channel?

If you have an indirect marketing channel, how can you make sure the right message is being sent? How can you better support your marketing channels to sell more of your product?

What is your overall business model? Does it work well in the current market? You will need to constantly analyze your business model to make sure it is still relevant as the market changes.

Example 8: Girl Scouts United States

The girl scouts had two objectives with this campaign: the primary objective was to engage alumni and to begin to develop a network of donors for future campaigns. The secondary objective was to gather donations from those women who were ready to donate, and to build a database of new alumni.

The campaign took advantage of the following mediums:

- Direct mail
- Email (initial and follow-up)
- Web—Personalized landing pages
- Social Media (Facebook Cause page, YouTube Video)
- Telesales follow up

The direct mail piece was versioned by segment and featured prominent women of the community that had been Girl Scouts. The call to action drove recipients to a personalized involvement site via a PURL:

**Age group segment
20–39**

Jane, the sash was there for you, now make sure it is there for all daughters.

Girl Scouts developed your pursuit of achievement, optimism and confidence. Guarantee the same for today's girls by supporting Girl Scouts.

Please log onto your personalized involvement site today and learn how you can help in these urgent times. Girl Scouts need you.
Support the sash. Support her future.

www.JaneSample.supportthesash.o

Girl Scouts.
Arizona Cactus-Pine Council, Inc.
119 East Coronado Road
Phoenix, AZ 85004
602.452.7077 • 1 800 352.6133 ext. 7077

Jane, Support the Sash

Support the Sash

**Age group segment
40–49**

Jane, as part of the most successful generation, many of the skills you use every day were learned in Girl Scouting.

Invest in the success of today's girls by supporting Girl Scouts. These may be challenging times, but investing in girls gives a return that is priceless.

Please log onto your personalized involvement site today and learn how you can help in these urgent times. Girl Scouts need you now more than ever.
Support the sash. Support her future.

www.JaneSample.supportthesash.org

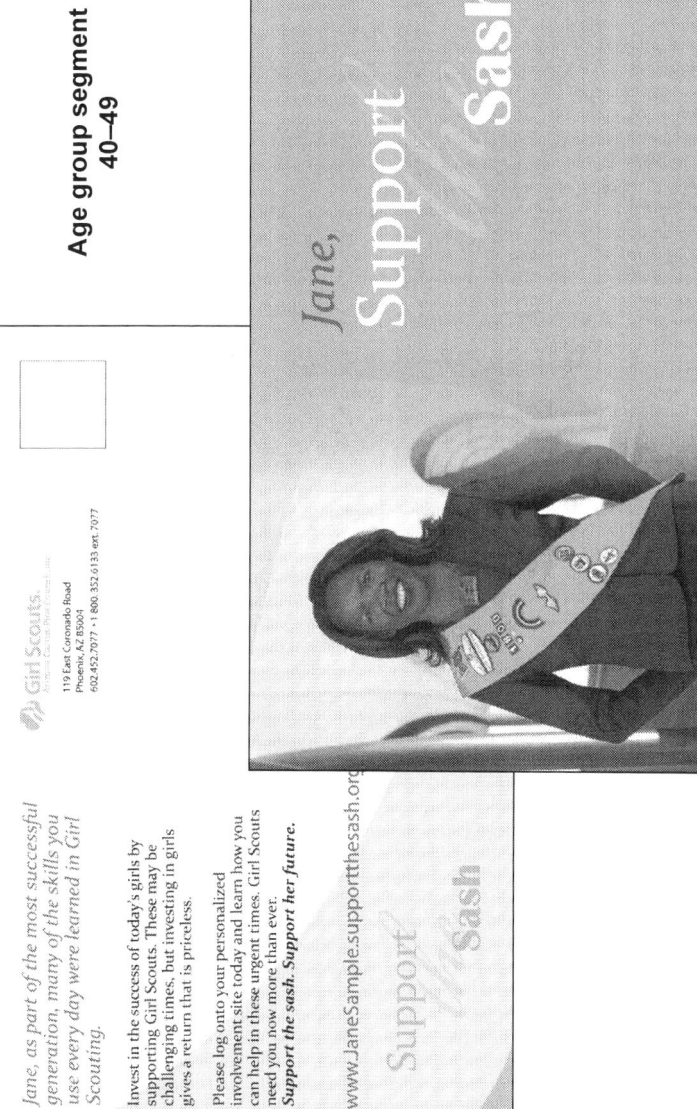

Girl Scouts.
119 East Coronado Road
Phoenix, AZ 85004
602.452.7077 • 1.800.352.6133 ext. 7077

Jane,
Support the Sash

The Digital & Direct Marketing Goose   85

**Age group segment
50–59**

Jane, the ideals you learned as a young Girl Scout shaped the world.

Today, millions of Girl Scouts follow in your footsteps, ready to address the challenges around us. Please support them with a generous gift to Girl Scouting. During these difficult times, the Girl Scout sisterhood has never been more important.

Please log onto your personalized involvement site and tell us how you can help in these urgent times. Girl Scouts need you now more than ever. **Support the Sash. Secure her future.**

www.JaneSample.supportthesash.org

Girl Scouts
119 East Coronado Road
Phoenix, AZ 85004
602.452.7077 • 1.800.352.6133 ext.7077

Support *the* Sash

Jane,
Support *the* Sash

Age group segment
60+

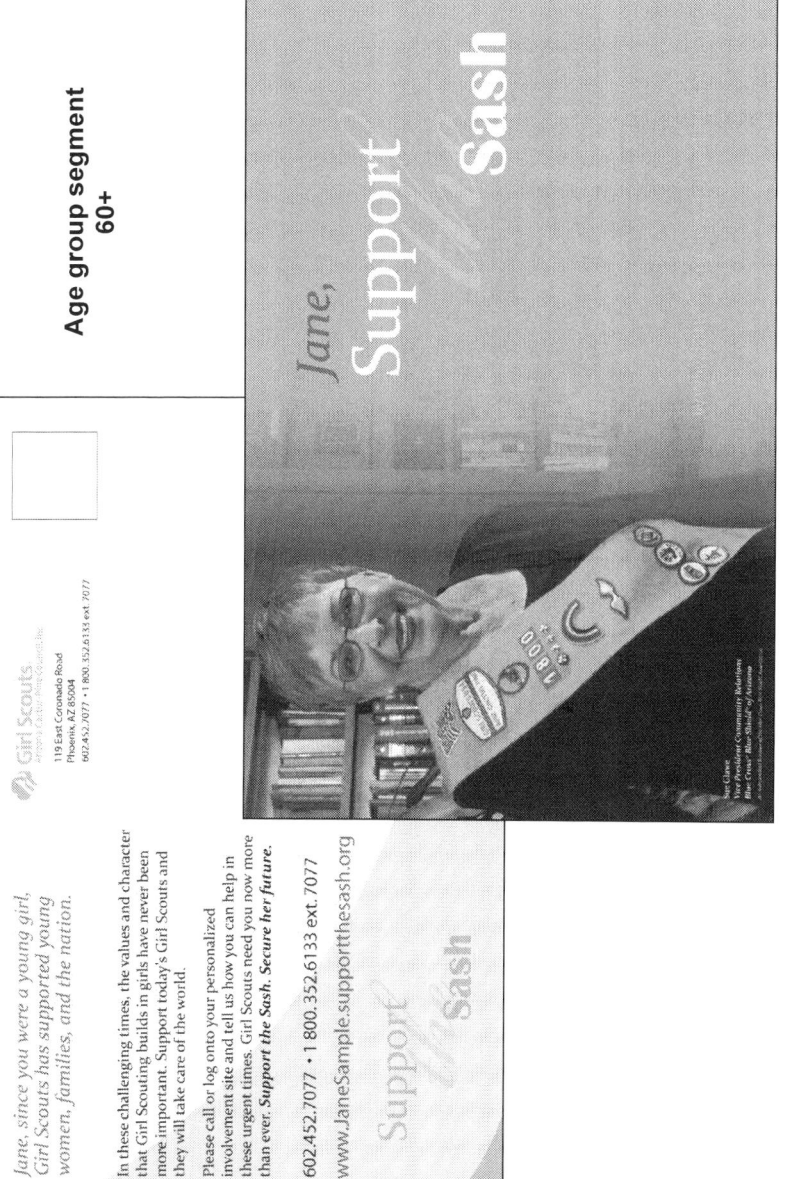

Jane, since you were a young girl, Girl Scouts has supported young women, families, and the nation.

In these challenging times, the values and character that Girl Scouting builds in girls have never been more important. Support today's Girl Scouts and they will take care of the world.

Please call or log onto your personalized involvement site and tell us how you can help in these urgent times. Girl Scouts need you now more than ever. *Support the Sash. Secure her future.*

602.452.7077 • 1 800.352.6133 ext. 7077
www.JaneSample.supportthesash.org

Girl Scouts
119 East Coronado Road
Phoenix, AZ 85004
602.452.7077 • 1 800.352.6133 ext 7077

Jane,
Support the Sash

Sue Glawe
Vice President Community Relations
Blue Cross / Blue Shield of Arizona

A campaign email was sent to all alumni for whom the council had email addresses. This email was timed to arrive the same day as the direct mail piece. The call to action drove recipients to their personalized involvement site via the same PURL as the direct mail piece.

Follow-up emails were sent to individuals who visited their PURL and asked them to refer a friend and join the GSACPC Facebook page. Non-responders received an email encouraging them to visit their PURL.

The personalized involvement site was versioned by segment and provided compelling copy that would resonate with each age group. Visitors were asked to make a donation to help "Support the Sash."

Those who indicated an interest in making a donation were sent to a site that would allow them to complete a secure online transaction. After they hit the donation site, a representative would follow up with a phone call. In most cases, this was to thank them for their donation. In some instances, if visitors noted that they would like to make a gift, but had not done so online, the representative called and asked them if they preferred to donate in a different manner.

Respondents who did not want to donate right away were offered other avenues to get involved. This was part of a strategy that would cultivate future donations by keeping the women engaged. A "refer a friend" function enabled these alumni to invite others to participate in the campaign through an automated email.

Alumni were also encouraged to join a Facebook Cause page for the GSACPC. This page was designed to create an online community in an environment that would allow ongoing conversations and future donations. The service provider helped set up the Facebook page, which is being maintained by GSACPC.

A YouTube video was also uploaded to create awareness of the campaign and drive incremental involvement in the Facebook Cause page.

"Case study source: *http://www.podi.org/casestudy*, a collection of over 500 successful digital and direct marketing solutions in full color."

Tip 9: Set Goals and Key Performance Indicators, and Use Resources Effectively

Your goal should be a number based on what you want to achieve. This number represents your desired ultimate result and is always measurable. If your goal is not a number, it is more likely an objective or even an activity of an objective. If you initially set your goal for something that is not a number, ask yourself, "Why do I want to achieve that?" In all likelihood, it will relate to a number such as X number of unit sales, revenue, profit, or earnings growth. That number will be the actual goal.

Once you establish your goals, you need to define the strategy that will help you get there. A strategy is what you think needs to happen in order for you to attain your goals. Don't confuse a goal with a strategy. I once heard someone say, "Our strategy for this year is to have our yearly sales target done by end of Q2." That statement represents a goal, not a strategy, and it also should be quantified with a number. A better statement would be, "Our goal is to sell $100 million by end of Q2," and the strategy should relate to how you would achieve that.

Strategies consist of objectives and activities that also relate to your goals. Activities support objectives, while objectives support goals.

People make statements such as, "My goal is to improve market perception." This, however, would not be the goal. It is an objective that would support a goal, such as increasing revenue by X% or selling X number of units. To fulfill that objective, there would be a series of activities, such as marketing campaigns. An example of this series would be a marketing campaign (activity) that helped improve market perception (objective), which in turn helped you hit a $1 million in sales (goal).

Setting up the right objectives is a critical part of the strategy because not even the best campaign activity will help you hit your goals if your objectives are wrong. As I mentioned before, you should perform a SWOT analysis before you set up your objectives. Strengths and Weaknesses relate to your company and products or services; Opportunities and Threats relate to the market to which you are selling. Again, it is critical to set up the right goals to have a good chance at building a successful strategy that will help you achieve those goals.

Working in this detailed and structured manner will increase your focus and the chances of better campaigns.

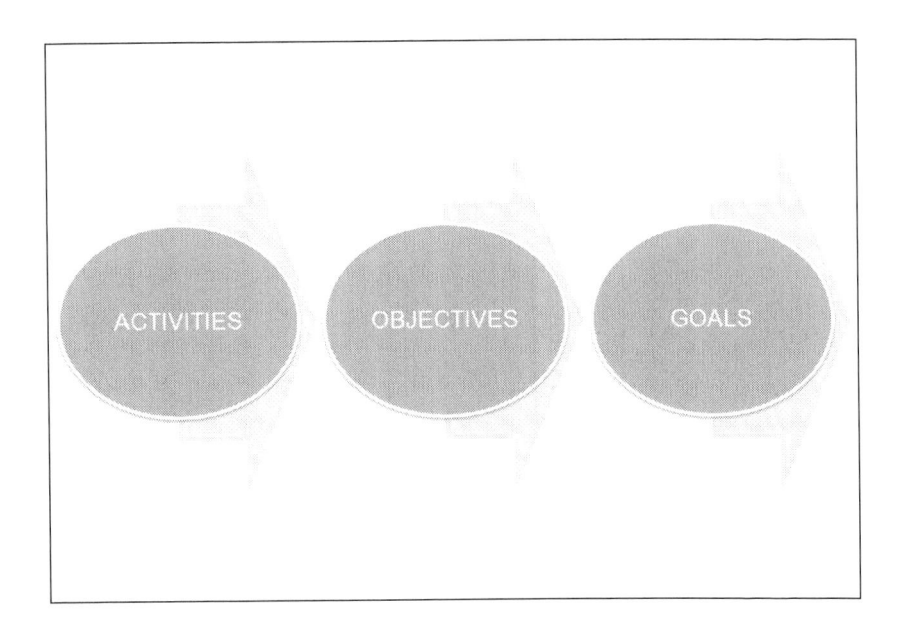

ACTIVITIES   OBJECTIVES   GOALS

Make sure your goals are realistic. If they are too high, you will not get enough support, as you will not be seen as credible. If they are too low, the people around you will likely be insufficiently motivated, and you will not realize your sales potential.

Key Performance Indicators (KPIs)

KPIs are quantifiable measurements. They are defined up front and are used to measure your program's success or failure in relation to your marketing activities. Some common KPIs include response rates, closing rates, sales, gross profit ration, etc.

Use Your Resources Effectively

Your budget and partners are the two main things you need to look at to determine your resources. How you invest your marketing budget is critical for a better ROMI. It is not only crucial how much you spend, but how well you spend it. Historically, marketing spending has been about the quantity of impact. Today, the quality of the impact is quickly becoming more important.

In the past, if you had $50,000 to spend, the first thing you did was look at your target audience. As previously discussed, it was always "bigger is better" in terms of the target. So to make an easy calculation, let's say you wanted to reach a potential target group of 50,000 consumers and you knew you could only afford to spend an average of $1 per consumer.

Today, this process can be quite different. Instead of looking at the total number of consumers in your target group, you must determine how much to invest to capture the attention of one consumer and have a chance to complete the sale with them. Estimating the cost to make a sale is essential here. If the answer is $10, you divide your marketing budget of $50,000 by $10, and this tells you that you can afford to talk to 5,000 people with the money that you have.

The analysis is not about making a low-cost contact with many people (unless it makes sense), but to impress the ones you do contact, giving them enough good reasons to buy from you. When relevant, it is more effective to invest $10 per potential buyer and have a chance at selling your products to 5,000 people than investing $1 and having no chance to sell your product to 50,000.

As an additional benefit, targeted customers of quality marketing are more likely to be impressed by your efforts, and they will probably tell others about your offering. Word of mouth is extremely effective. In the end, the best way to reach the original target of 50,000 people may be to do a proper job with the 5,000 you can afford to contact.

Do not try to do more than you can afford. A well-planned and well-executed campaign with a limited budget that hits only some potential buyers is much better than a campaign that is planned incorrectly and reaches many people in an inefficient way.

Using partners to contribute to your strategy is a good way to improve your marketing results. Your partners could be internal and external. Often you will build your initial strategy based on using both internal and external partners where they will be most effective. You might have existing partners with heavy consumer traffic in their own online and brick-and-mortar shops, or partners that can help you with the planning and execution of your marketing campaign.

Here are some questions to ask about your existing partners:

- Can they help you identify your target groups in their shops?
- Can they help you collect useful information?
- Can they make your product stronger and more valuable?
- Can they help you make your pitch more relevant?

And don't forget the reverse: What can you do to help your partners in return?

Example 9: Kodak Spain

Here is an example where Kodak partnered with Estudios Durero to create a campaign that invested more time and marketing budget with fewer companies in order to better capture their attention and show them value. This is also a good example of using multiple channels—some new, some old—with great success.

Kodak wanted target prospects for a digital printing press it was displaying at a graphic arts show in Barcelona, Spain. To make their prospects feel valued and special and to capture their attention, the company invested in a nice gift box. Prospects were asked about how they were going to get to the show and about their favorite city in Spain. Fifty percent of the prospects responded to the first mailer.

A second mailer was sent out to those prospects that had responded with personalized images related to the mode of transportation they'd indicated that they would use to come to the show. Images of roads, train stations, and airports were personalized with the prospect's name. It also contained an image of their favorite city in Spain with a message that they could win an all-expenses-paid trip to that city if they attended the Kodak event taking place at the graphic arts show.

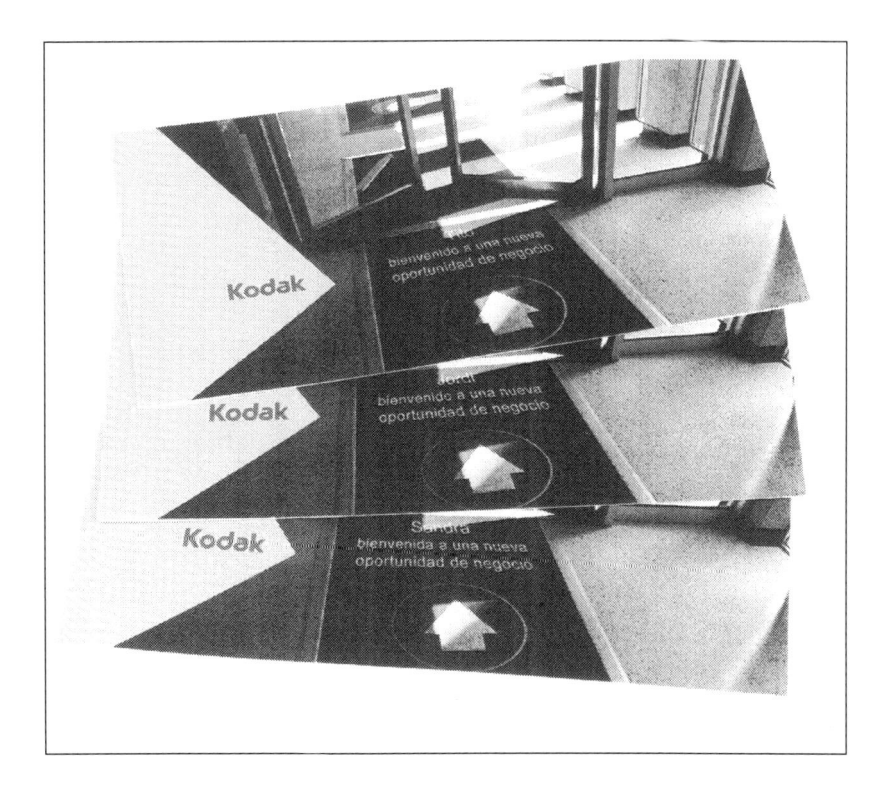

Now that they had a commitment from the prospects, in order to keep the momentum going, a personalized email was sent out informing prospects of convenient days to visit Kodak's event, which included an agenda and the food menu for the event.

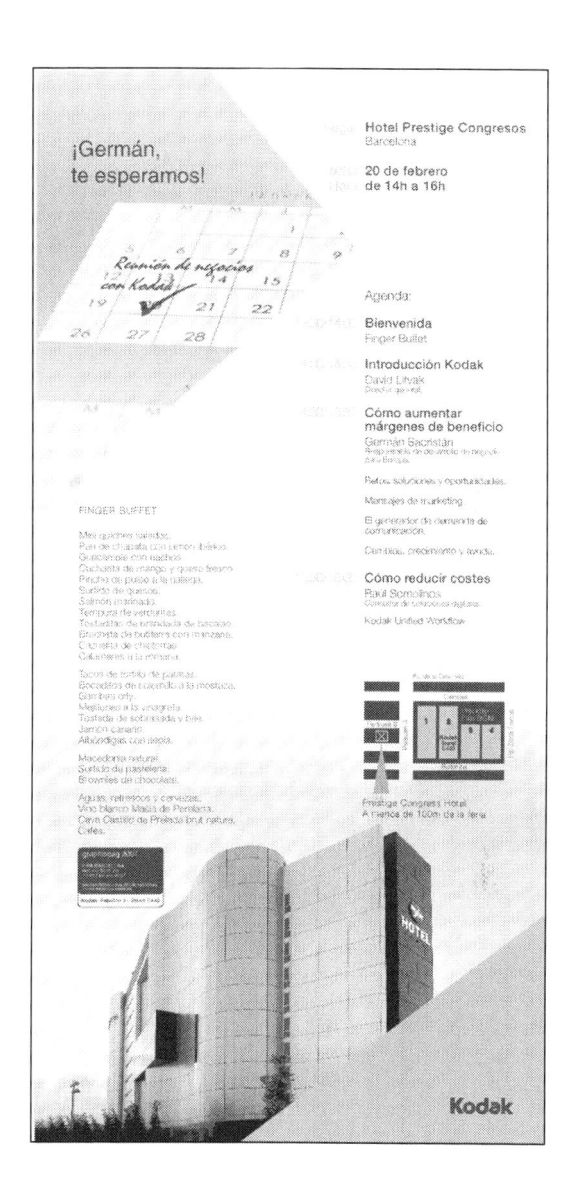

Finally, an SMS message was sent out to the prospect two hours before the Kodak event reminding them to come.

Not only did Kodak have a 50% response rate, they didn't lose one prospect along the way. Everyone that responded that they would attend did so.

"Case study source: http://www.podi.org/casestudy, a collection of over 500 successful digital and direct marketing solutions in full color."

Tip 10
Proper Creation of Target Profiles Is Imperative to Be Successful

It is more difficult to build a campaign for digital and direct marketing than for generic marketing. Generic marketing only requires one profile based on average target demographic information and generic buying criteria. For digital and direct marketing, we need to create as many profiles that make sense and find the potential buyers that fit those profiles.

Describing and segmenting, or profiling, your target is a very critical step in your strategy. Your goal is to effectively reach out to your target with relevant marketing pieces that will make them want to buy from you.

You describe your target based on what you sell and where you sell it. There are four critical steps to help you describe your target:

- Look at your product and brand strengths and weaknesses and value proposition, including USPs.

- Look at your market opportunities and threats.

- Analyze who is buying what from you, who is not, and why.

- Do some market research if necessary.
    a. Test with the people that you think are your target to make sure they really are.

In the past, you only had to do the step above of describing your target before you started to pitch to them with the same message, creativity, and channel. Today, in order to capture the attention of your target and be relevant in your communication, you need to segment or profile your target, which means adding an extra step to your marketing strategy. The main purpose of segmenting and profiling your target is to create the blueprint that will help you organize your customers into different groups or profiles so you can improve your relevance and therefore your sales productivity, while communicating with each one of them. You will segment and profile your target based on what is important to know from potential buyers in order to become more relevant when communicating with them:

- You will need to know some personal characteristics of your target audience such as age, gender, etc. that are relevant to what you sell. Knowing those characteristics will help you communicate in a more personal and effective way.

- It will also be helpful to create profiles based on the different reasons they would buy your products or services (buying criteria). Analyzing your CRM is extremely helpful on this step.

- It's also relevant to profile based on the type of products or services that your target has already bought, when, where, and how they bought them. Keep track of what your customers buy, when, where and how.

Profiles will drive what you need to say, when, and how you say it in your next marketing program. Describing and segmenting or profiling your target is so critical that if you do it wrong the campaign will fail. You need to make sure you are talking to the right people, at the right time, and in the right way to be successful. You create your profiles based on:

1. Who could buy my product(s)?
2. Why do they buy each product?

3. What did they already buy and when and how often do they make purchases?
4. Where do they buy products/services?
5. How do they buy products? And how do they prefer to be contacted?

1. Who could buy my product(s)?

What does my target audience look like for each product or service that I want to sell? What is important to know from them? This is where you start building the profiles. Some typical attributes that describe customers' profiles are:

- Age
- Gender
- Marital status (married, single, divorced, widow, widower)
- Life stage (adolescent, student, just married, working career, retired)
- Postal/ZIP code, city, country
- Languages, cultures, religions
- Career (job, industry, studies, schools)
- Earnings
- Hobbies (vacations, sports, etc.)
- Political tendency

Remember that you only need to know what will help you be more relevant to sell your product or service.

Are there other relevant indicators? What else will help you be more relevant when communicating to your target groups? Examples might include books, newspapers, and magazines they read, movies and programs they watch, music they listen to, whether or not they have pets, height, weight, whether or not they wear glasses, etc.

Life changes are another important consideration in marketing. Changing jobs, relocating homes and moving from one country to another, having a baby, retirement, etc., are all emotional and sometimes stressful events and make people more disposed to buy. These are opportunities to help fill a special or new-found need. For example, people that are having a baby are not only in the market for baby food; they might also be in the market for a bigger car or a new house for the larger family. You might find less competition when targeting a group this way.

In the case of B2B, you will have to describe not only the profile of the company that will buy your product, but also that of the person making the buying decision within that company.

2. Why do they buy each product?

People buy products for different reasons. These reasons define the various buying criteria and further shape the different profiles. The reasons will be driven by your product's specs or features and different models, and also by your USPs and your company's values and perception.

If you don't know your customer's buying criteria sometimes you can create assumptions. Assumptions could be made like this: "The buying criteria or reasons that a 23-year-old single male that lives in New York City who already buys Product X from me would also buy Product Y are A, B and C." Be very careful when speculating about people and stereotypes. This will work for some products and some scenarios, but not for all.

There may also be very different reasons why individuals have the same buying criteria. For example, two people may buy a car for the all-wheel-drive (AWD) system, which would be their buying criteria. However, individual A may want AWD because he skis and often drives in the snow, while individual B may want it because he likes to hunt up in the mountains. The buying criteria here are the same for both, but the reasons behind their reason for buying are different. This difference will obviously affect the content of your marketing pieces, and it is critical to be aware of it.

3. What did they already buy and when and how often do they make purchases?

Knowing what other products and/or services your customers already have will help you be more effective when trying to cross sell and up sell to them. This will help you increase the customer value to your business.

One of the easiest and more effective ways to profile existing customers is by size and frequency of purchase. You should never spend the same marketing money with every profile, nor should you use the same strategy.

Every business in the market has these four types of customers or profiles:

Customer A: They buy a lot and often. You can't afford to lose these customers. An aggressive loyalty program might be called for here.

Customer B: They buy a lot, but not too often. The strategy here could be building relationships to make this group visit us more often.

Customer C: They buy little, but often. Maybe they do not know your entire portfolio. Cross and up selling might be a good strategy for this target group.

Customer D: They buy little and not very often. We need to identify this group and not invest too much in them. There are, of course, always exceptions.

To have more effective communication with the customer groups above, you could even further profile the different individuals or companies in each customer group.

In addition, depending on the product(s) that you sell, it may be easier to predict when consumers will buy. For example, consumers buy vacation packages around the same time every year. Study your customer relationship management (CRM) carefully to identify when your customers are more likely to buy from you. Analyzing the timing of your customers' purchases is critical to be able to target them at the right time as well as identify customers that have not purchased from you when they were due to. The latter may be an indication that they switched to one of your competitors. You can then follow up with them to identify why and/or offer incentives that may help you win them back.

4. Where do they buy products/services?

Today consumers have two choices with regards to where they want buy from you: online or offline. Understanding where your customers would like to buy from you will help you drive them to the place where they feel more comfortable, increasing your chances of success. At the same time, defining where customers buy your product(s) can also help you decide which channel(s) to use in your communications.

5. How do they buy products? And how do they prefer to be contacted?

In order to determine how do your customers buy, it will be helpful to know their buying behavior and habits. A well-organized and up-to-date CRM system can help you analyze who bought what products from you and how they bought them.

Studying your customer's history will help you further define your different profiles and will also help you place your customers in the correct ones.

You can also profile your customers based on how they want to be contacted. What are their preferred channels? These channels may not be the most convenient for you, but you must use the ones your customers and prospects like. These include traditional as well as digital channels. Choosing the right channels when communicating with your prospects will increase your chances of a sale.

Sub-Segment as Needed

You will have to sub-segment, or drill down the target profiles, as much as necessary to have the best chance at selling your product. The more precise the profile and the more accurate your information, the better you'll be able to customize not only your message, but also the entire marketing piece and communication channel. But how much can you afford to spend (in time, money and effort) on what you want to know?

Continually finding and updating information about an individual or company in your target group must not cost you more than the value of that individual as a customer. Sometimes you simply have to work with what you have. You don't always need to pay for the information you don't have because it might be relatively easy to predict based on what you already know about someone. Sensitivity and experience can help you make low-risk assumptions.

Customer Relationship Management (CRM)

The CRM system is the tool that will help you keep relevant information about your customers in an organized way. In order to create an effective and functional CRM, you need to focus on quality of information vs. quantity. A functional CRM system should always be organized by what you need to know to sell your products or services. By doing so, you can easily identify what information is missing about each customer, and encourage other sales and marketing channels to feed that information into the system so you can better profile each customer. Your CRM needs to be well connected to all of your marketing and sales activities and channels so the relevant information can be easily uploaded and used. A thoughtfully organized CRM will provide focus and direction to the people and departments within your organization. It is imperative for them to understand not only what information you need, but also how it will be used and what the personal value will be to them and their departments. Demonstrating the value of the CRM in this way will drive use of the CRM and the timely feeding of the proper information into the system. If the CRM is established correctly from the beginning, it will be a valuable tool for ongoing marketing needs.

This hard, upfront work of properly setting up your CRM as a functional tool will pay off by helping you better profile your customers and in return, drive the success of your future campaigns.

The main four reasons of having and analyzing a CRM are:

- To describe your target by looking at the customers that already buy from you.

- To increase customer value by up-sell and cross-sell to your existing customers.

- To make intelligent assumptions about buying criteria, customer's behavior and habits by knowing what people buy, when, where, why and how.

- To classify your customers in different profiles by knowing what is important to know from them.

Some people think that the right way to create good profiles is just by analyzing the data in your CRM. Unfortunately, this is not 100% correct. Analyzing why some people are buying some products and others aren't might help you describe your target, but not necessarily profile it the right way. Be very careful here. Just because a customer is not buying from you doesn't mean she/he is not a potential customer, but perhaps you are failing to communicate with that particular customer. Data is powerful, but if not properly balanced with common sense and experience it may lead you in the wrong direction.

As discussed before, in order to create the right profiles you need to start defining what it is important to know from your target based on what you sell and where you sell it. Then you will go to your CRM to see if there is anything you've forgotten that is important to add to your profiles. Making profiles only with the information that you have in your CRM will limit yourself for the simple reason that what you know might not be enough to create the right profiles.

A simple example of creating good profiles could be that after I analyze the data in my CRM I come to the conclusion that my target is middle class people (male and female) that can drive and have kids. I just described my target, but now I have to profile it or segment it. I might come to the conclusion that it is important for me to know their age, gender, if they are married or divorce, gender of kids and age, income and the type of car they drive. Then I will create my profiles based on that.

I might think that it is also important to know if my target buys on or offline and what time of the year they are more likely to buy. Then I will add that to my profiling. This can get as complicated as I need to be as I can also decide that it is critical to know buying criteria and customer's behavior and habits to be even more relevant when I engage my target. In order to do that, I will have to define what are the different buying criteria when someone buys my products as well as the different customer's behaviors and habits. Knowing what people buy, when, where, why and how could help you make intelligent assumptions about buying criteria and customer's behavior and habits.

Transactional data can help you better understand your customers. You probably won't have transactional data about your customers unless you're offering them financial services. Some retail businesses offer credit card services to their customers to make it easier to buy from them and also to profit from these financial services. In the process, they are building critical information about their existing customers. Knowing what people buy, when they buy, where they buy it and how much they pay for it is priceless information that will help you better profile your customers. Transactional data can also be built through loyalty cards and incentives.

You can do two levels of profiling based on the information you have about the people and/or companies in your CRM. You might have a more detailed and diverse profile for existing customers than for prospects since you may have transactional purchasing information about a customer that you do not have about a prospect. It's still very critical to profile prospects as well so that you have a better chance at convincing them to become customers. As an example, a simple prospect profile can be females from 30 to 40 years of age that live in an area where the average income is $80,000 per year vs. a more detailed profile that includes 30 to 40 year old females that live in an area where the average income is $80,000 per year that buy certain products online in the summer months.

A good process for a successful campaign could be:

1. After describing your target, create the different profiles based on what you sell, the market where you sell it, and the information that you need from your target in order to be able to sell to them.

2. Look at the data that you have in your CRM to see if you can add anything to your profiles and if you have enough information to classify your customers in the right profiles. Sometimes you might not have all the data, but enough to make low risk intelligent assumptions that will help you classify your customers. Knowing the age, address, and gender of someone might help you make low risk assumptions about income and buying criteria.

3. If you don't have enough information to place your customers in the right profiles, you will have to engage them to build that information.

4. Once every customer is in the right profile, engage them with promotional offers that are relevant to each of them.

Customize your marketing piece to a level that is appropriate, but don't overdo it because the recipient might find it invasive. The level of customization will be determined by the definition of the profile. Sometimes a little customization works better than too much. Neither is it a case of the more profiles you create, the better. You need to decide what is good enough and go from there. What you sell, where you sell it, and what you need to know from potential buyers to sell it will guide you in the number of profiles you need to create. Sometimes creating a few simple profiles works better than creating many.

There is nothing new about describing and profiling a target—salespeople have been doing it for hundreds of years. Successful salespeople describe their target based on what they sell and where before they go and visit anyone. As discussed in Tip 8, they think about their products, services, brand and even their own strengths and weaknesses. Then they will think about their market opportunities and threats. A quick SWOT analysis will help them describe their target. Then they will determine what they have to know from their target market in order to be relevant when trying to sell to them. That is how they will eventually profile their customers. After going through this preparation phase, they will go and visit their target, but will not execute their final pitch until they have enough information to profile the customer. In order to do that, they will ask relevant questions and pay attention to any other relevant information they discover. In marketing, it is more difficult because we can't see the people that we are communicating with so we are limited to less information.

Effective salespeople have one obvious goal when approaching customers and that is to sell them something. They achieve that goal by focusing on two main objectives; one is to build relevant information that will help them profile the customer so they can adapt their pitch to that particular customer, and the second is trying to build good relationships while doing so. Salespeople can do it on the fly and individually, as their target audience is relatively small. Conversely, in marketing, targets are often very large. Even though the strategy of segmentation and profiling is the same, we do it in a more mechanical way also using the most appropriate digital technologies. Profiling allows you to personalize or version your marketing piece depending who you are talking to. Therefore, effective marketers need to have a different set of skills in order to be successful. They need to have experience selling face-to-face before they can be successful at direct marketing using the latest digital communication channels.

Here are some different product and market scenarios that may affect your profiling:

- Well-known products where you have strong USPs and little competition might need less work and, therefore, less profiling.

- On the other hand, selling commodity products in competitive markets means you need to work harder at convincing someone to buy from you. Therefore, you might need more profiling within your target group in order to be even more targeted and relevant.

- Economic recessions mean that fewer people are buying, so you must adjust your profiles based on current market conditions.

- Products with many separate features lead to a greater diversity of buying criteria, again requiring more profiling.

Profiling for B2B is slightly different than B2C. For B2B, you will have to profile the company as well as the person or people responsible for purchasing your products and/or services and their influencers. The methodology is the same. You will have to ask yourself what you need to know from companies and people that will help you be more relevant when communicating with them. The positive in B2B is that it is often easier to pull information about a company than a person.

Summary: Important Points to Remember

Create profiles based on what you sell, where you sell it, and what is important to know from potential buyers to sell it. Having relevant information about your customers and prospects will help you place them in the right profile. Knowing your customers well will help you quickly identify similar individuals in the market. Having the right individual or company in the right profile will help make your marketing piece more relevant and, in turn, help your sales.

- Customer profiles give you focus and direction.

- Customer profiles define the different target groups you need to reach.

- Customer profiles are critical when creating the messaging, choosing the channel, and building creativity.

- You will build your communication strategy based on the profiles that you have created.

- Personal experience, CRM systems, and analytics help you create better campaigns.

- Going through the analytics might also identify opportunities where you can improve your product/service.

- Looking at existing satisfied and unsatisfied customers will help you better describe your target.

- There is nothing new about profiling. We have been doing it for hundreds of years. Good salespeople visited customers and profiled them before they made their final pitch. The difference then was that we did it face-to-face and one-to-one, while today we need to communicate one to many in order to increase sales productivity.

- Your products or services and the market, including your customers/prospects and competitors, are constantly changing. Make sure you continually update what is important to know, as well as your customer profiles.

Example 10: Citadel United States

Citadel is a college with a foundation that is charged with finding donors for athletic scholarships. The Kennickell Group helped them with a new marketing program. They had the following data information:

- Year of graduation
- Sports played
- Education major
- Donors
- Military rank
- + Traditional data

After analyzing their data they came to the following conclusions:

- Members are located closer to the campus (75 to 100 miles).
- Memberships become more likely as military rank increases.
- A membership could rise 4 times if the alumni played any sports.

Previous notions were:

- Athletic were not donors.
- Military rank has no influence.
- Distance has no effect.
- No difference between men and women.

A new profiling was developed after the new findings. Thanks to the analytics, Citadel now is talking to the right people which in return will increase their chances of more successful campaigns.

Tip 11
You Need An Effective Data Collection Strategy to Win

Now that you have defined the segments or profiles, you need to start populating or classifying each customer into the appropriate profile so that you can take the corresponding actions when communicating with them. You can't classify your customers in the appropriate profiles without information about them:

You either have information or you don't. If you don't, you have to buy it or build it, and both cost money:

- You buy information either directly from the consumers, or, if you can't buy the required personal information from the individuals you wish to target, from a company that sells that information. These companies will sell you data, including demographic information, based on where your target lives. Even though this is not the precise information about each individual you want to target, it is good enough to increase your chances of being more relevant. This will help you to either sell them your products or collect more relevant information from them through better interactions.

- You build information through market engagement and research:
1. You need to first describe your market engagement channels:
   a. Human: Customer Service & Hotlines, Technical Service, Billing, Direct and Indirect Sales Channels, telemarketing, on and offline communities and social events.
   b. Non-Human: Online Shops, directly or indirectly (publications), on and offline marketing communication campaigns.

   As discussed before, make sure your CRM is well connected to all of your marketing and sales activities and channels so the relevant information can be easily uploaded and used.

2. Then you need a market engagement plan to constantly retrieve relevant information:

   a. When the market comes to you:

   Customers will contact you through your call center, your customer or technical service department, your billing, or even your salesforce. This is a good opportunity to collect relevant information to feed into your CRM, while addressing the purpose of their call. (The primary effort in this case should be addressing the reason for their call, so as to not be annoying or obvious in your attempts to collect the additional information.) Make sure you train human channels on how to pull customer information and set up an incentive plan for them to do so.

   In the case of potential buyers visiting your online and/or offline shops, any interaction will also provide a great opportunity to identify and place them in the right profiles. Many marketers are very excited that they have thousands of visits every day or week to their online shops. My question to them is always the same: "Who are those online visitors, and what do they want?" Often they can't tell me. These people have come to your site for a reason, and you are missing a great opportunity if you do not try to engage them and gather information on who they are and why they are there. A good incentive plan will help you identify them and a proper online tracking strategy will help you find out why they are there. A simple example would be offering visitors a chance to enter a drawing for a free trip to Bermuda. In order to enter, they will have to register and tell you who they are. You might even include other relevant basic questions in the registration form that will help you better profile them. Now that you know who they are, you can also track them online to see where they go and what they read. That will help you profile potential buyers in more detail. Even if only a small percentage of visitors respond to the incentive, you have added very relevant prospects, which you now know, to your target list.

Websites are great for retrieving information from visitors. To do so in a successful way, you may have to reorganize your website from product oriented, to need/profile oriented in order to gather the best information from your visitors. If you have a product-oriented site and you are tracking your visitors, you will only know which products they are interested in. This is a good start, but if, on the other hand, you are able to organize your site by customer needs and profiles, you will not only know which product might suit their profile or need, but also why. It is more valuable to know that someone is interested in safety, space, and cost when it comes to a car purchase rather than simply knowing they looked at a Ford Focus. You can make assumptions as to why a person looked at that car, but if you know her/his needs and profile you know exactly why. This will allow for more tailored communication with the ability to recommend additional products that fit their interest or profile. Having more information about the visitors gives you more control.

There is nothing new about this idea—good salespeople do it all the time. They identify your profile while interacting with you and start making intelligent suggestions or recommendations that fit that profile. They will do this with sensitivity. However, if you do organize your site by profile it is, similarly, best to take a subtle approach. Don't be too obvious, as being confronted by a navigation grid that lists a user's personal characteristics (age, salary, etc.) may be seen as intrusive and cause potential buyers to leave. The same navigation represented by helpful questions ("If you are concerned with X click here.") will be seen as helpful and time saving while still allowing you to identify a prospect's profile and make intelligent and valuable recommendations.

If your data collection is more overt, you will either need to provide incentives to the visitors or clearly show enough value for them to be willing to provide that information to you. The most important pieces of information that you need to collect from visitors are about who they are and what they want. An incentive can be a gift or relevant information that is valued by your visitors. If they have visited your online shop, it is most likely because they are interested in some of the products that you sell or services that you offer, therefore your incentive could be relevant to what you sell. For example, a company that sells vacation packages could offer a drawing to win a free trip.

This also applies to your offline shops. For example, I know of a telecommunication company that has interactive marketing screens in their shops for customers that are waiting for a sales representative during peak hours. Unfortunately, this company was not capturing information on their customers' interactions and behaviors on these screens. This was a huge opportunity lost. A percentage of these customers would leave without ever talking to a sales representative, and the company lost the chance to gather any information on them about who they were, what they wanted, and how they could be contacted for follow up. If they collected information, the company could then contact them with a direct mailer apologizing for not personally helping them while they were in the shop, while also making it up to them with an incentive to buy, such as a discount on an item they were looking at on the screen. This provides a great opportunity to increase sales productivity. Regular sales reps could also gather relevant information from their visitors while interacting with them.

b. When you go to contact the market:

You will also need to approach individuals, companies, and communities that fit your target description to gather information from them.

You can approach them in several ways:

- Face-to-face sales

- Telemarketing

- Regular campaigns, both online and offline

- Social media

- Before you approach potential buyers you will need to answer these four critical questions:
- How do you capture their attention?
- What are the incentives that will convince them to give you the information that you want?
- How many times do you have to contact them, and what do you have to tell them each time to obtain the information you need?
- Which communication channels will you use to contact them?
- Make sure you direct your potential buyer to the places where it is easiest for them to provide information and easiest for you to collect it.

Social media is a great tool for retrieving information from your potential buyer so you can follow up with them in a more relevant manner. There will be more on social media later on in this book.

As a summary of your data collection strategy, make sure you set up incentive plans to encourage your human customer engagement channels as well as your offline and online customers to provide information to you. Set up a strategy to follow customers online and offline. When trying to retrieve information from your customers, make sure you utilize all the relevant communication channels or enablers and integrate them when appropriate. For example, you might send a direct mailer to someone containing a QR code that will lead them to an online registration site where you can build information about a particular customer. Do not forget to link your engagement channels (human & non human) to your CRM.

3. Market research is another relevant way to build information. The Internet helps us research the market better and quicker. You can research your customer's websites to retrieve information from them in the case of a B2B model. You can pull consumer information from social networks in the case of a B2C model.

Be sure to check the relevant data compliance laws in the country where you will launch the campaigns to make sure you are collecting, using, and safeguarding personal information properly.

Example 11: Walt Disney Parks and Resorts United States

The Walt Disney World Welcome Mailer is the first in a series of personalized and customized communications that are delivered to a guest in anticipation of their upcoming visit. The Call Center interacts with each guest and the specific details for every guest's upcoming visit are sent daily to RI Communications Group. The custom-created, personalized Welcome Mailer is generated and delivered to the guest within 48 hours.

The Welcome Mailer is designed to reinforce the guest's decision to take a Walt Disney World resort vacation and provides guests with only the information that is relevant to them and their travel party.

The details about each guest's visit triggers individualized recommendations for dining options, special events, entertainment, recreation, ticketed events, and other options.

The Welcome Mailer recognizes when a household is traveling as a family, party, group or individual and whether the guest is a new or repeat Walt Disney World resort visitor.

The personalized and customized Welcome Mailer exceeded goals for the reduction in the overall cancellation rate and an increase in ticket sales. The new Welcome Mailer was successful in driving incremental revenue for specific entertainment and event recommendations as compared with simply presenting information to guests about everything there is to do at a Walt Disney World park or resort.

Implementing this campaign required new tactics for the Call Center, building new cross-functional teams, asking new questions, and planning for a different experience for guests.

Your trip planning information

Welcome Sample Family

We're so happy you're coming back in March! Here's something special for your trip.

We want you to have the most magical vacation ever—after all, you're coming to the most magical place on earth. So, based on what you told us when you made your reservations, we've put together some information especially for you. Like answers to questions you didn't even know you had. Recommendations on not-to-be-missed shows and attractions. Even some things you might want to know since you're travelling with a child. We've also enclosed a Planning Checklist to keep everything on track. All to make getting ready for your upcoming *Walt Disney World®* vacation as fun and easy as it can be. And to help make sure you don't miss a minute of the magic.

Get ready for even more magic and fun—there's something extra special happening while you're here.

We're so thrilled you're coming back! You'll get to experience all your old favorites and see what's new in all four of our Theme Parks. In addition, this year we're celebrating the special magic that happens when friends and family gather together. *Magical Gatherings℠*. As you know, there's no better way for everyone of every age to find something just for them. So get ready to take home a whole new set of memories to treasure. We're ready to make your return visit as magical as possible.

Any Questions?
Call us at 407-W-DISNEY to plan any part of your vacation. Or simply log on to disneyworld.com.

Walk into the storybook fantasy of the Magic Kingdom® Park, one of our four Theme Parks.

There's a world of magic waiting for you. You're sure to find adventure around every corner... and there's no telling who you'll bump into.

You'll find a special kind of fun that brings everyone together.

Tip 11: You Need An Effective Data Collection Strategy to Win

More magic for the Sample Family!

Take a break with a recreation adventure that you'll never forget!

You'll find some great recreational activities here that are just perfect for an afternoon of fun. Enjoy state-of-the-art clay tennis courts. Take in a variety of water sports on one of our many lakes. Or choose world-class golf on tour-caliber courses. Kids love putting around our unique miniature golf courses. And they're always up for a day in the Water Parks and a splash down towering water slides. With so many different recreational activities all just steps away from your Resort, lots of good times await you.

If you're considering buying Theme Park tickets, you might want to switch to the package that gives you room, tickets and more!

Make the most of your stay with the *Ultimate Park Hopper* Ticket – it's exclusively for *Walt Disney World*® Resort hotel Guests. This ticket gives you unlimited access* to all four Theme Parks, water parks, and more for the length of your Resort stay. **You can save up to $66.00 by purchasing 3 adult (Ages 10+), 6-night *Ultimate Park Hopper* Tickets in advance, compared to buying the same tickets at your Resort.** When you call in advance for your tickets, also ask about the *Dream Maker*™ package, which gives you tickets and more for about the same price.
*Some activities/events may be separately priced.

Remember, for questions, you can call us at 407-W-DISNEY or call your Travel Agent. Or visit disneyworld.com for maps, ride descriptions and much more! You're on your way!

Sample A. Sample
123 Main Stret
New York, NY 10010-4930

Special trip planning information we've put together just for the Sample Family!

1-2OFV4Q

"Case study source: http://www.podi.org/casestudy, a collection of over 500 successful digital and direct marketing solutions in full color."

The Digital & Direct Marketing Goose

Tip 12
Successful Marketing Communication Engagement

Engaging your target audience in a relevant way will be much easier now that you have done your profiling. There are three very old and basic steps in sales and marketing engagement:

1. Capture the attention of your target.
2. Tell them what they want to hear not what you want to tell them.
3. Make it easy for them to buy from you or contact you.

1. The process of profiling provided you with great relevant information about your target. Now you can use that information to figure out how you are going to capture your customer's attention. You will capture your customer's attention with relevant messages, creativity, incentives, and the appropriate channels.

Technology also helps you to capture the attention of your target audience. Here are some great examples that illustrate just that:

*Good Sports used a technology that you can use to personalize images. In this case, you can see a text in the sky like it was made out of clouds.

*"Case study source: http://www.podi.org/casestudy, a collection of over 500 successful digital and direct marketing solutions in full color."

This dimensional print allows you to feel the orange texture as if it was real. It can be applied to other products, such as furniture or to any other product, including marketing pieces that feature scenery. Will this help you capture the attention of your target? I bet it will and they will also feel the value of your product just by touching the ad. Adding texture cannot only help you capture the attention of your target, but also get them excited about your products without even having to leave their homes.

How about sending a personalized thank-you note to your target wrapped around a chocolate bar? X1 in London did just that.

2. You need to tell your target what they want to know, which is not necessarily what you might want to tell them. They want to be reassured that you understand their problems and that you can help them solve them. This is not necessarily your standard marketing presentation. Some critical practices will include the following:

- Do not overwhelm your prospects with everything you know! Tell them only what is relevant to their needs. Also, just because you have good information about someone doesn't mean you are going to be successful at selling to them. Sensitivity is critical here. Successful salespeople know about you without letting on that they do, and they use that information subtly to sell you their products or services. Don't make it too obvious that you know what you know or you might scare your customers away. You have to use sensitivity and common sense based on what you sell and where you sell it in order to make the right move.

- Clearly demonstrate how your company can help your potential buyers with their specific problems.

After I searched online for help to do my taxes this year, I had a company following me on the internet for weeks. In this particular case to me, this was too much, too quick, too obvious, and too generic. They could only use a generic banner, which was far from addressing my personal needs because they didn't know anything about me. In this case, perhaps it would have worked better using an incentive to build more information about me that then they can use to be more relevant and helpful.

In other cases this could have worked well as a quick reminder of something that I am in the market for pushing me to make a buying decision.

- Sensitively use the potential buyer's profile information to tell them what they want to hear, and use your imagination, creativity, and channel to tell them in the manner that they want to hear it. Imagination and creativity will not only capture their attention, but will also help you show them the value of what you want to sell them in a way that will make them want to buy from you.

- Determine how many times you need to talk to your target in order to be able to demonstrate to them that you can fulfill their wants and needs. It usually takes more than one visit to get someone interested. It is also important to define the objective of each interaction.

- Make sure you establish the right relationships with your targets. Trust is needed to sell most products and services, and the proper relationships will help you build that trust.

- Pay attention to your prospects' buying process. What steps do they go through to make their purchase decision? They will be asking themselves questions such as: will I get the ROI I need? Will the product actually do what it's supposed to do? How will my decisions look to others?

- Don't forget to test your campaign with a few "experts" before you launch it. Consumers are the experts, as they tell us if we as marketers are right or wrong.

3. Now that you have captured your customer's attention and you have told them what they want to hear, you need to make it easy for them to buy from you or contact you. This may vary depending on whether you are in a B2B or B2C model. In most cases, prospects in a B2B model will have to contact you before they buy your product or service. If you operate under a B2C model, your customers might buy from you directly from your place of purchase without much personal interaction. Depending on the model that you are in, you should aim to make it easy for prospects to buy from you or contact you. If you do not make it easy for your prospects to buy from you or contact you when they are interested in your product, they will go somewhere else. You will have spent time and money to bring your customer to the point of purchase, only to lose them to a competitor due to a poor purchasing process. In another case, they might be tempted to buy and need a little push or incentive. Making it easy to buy from you is especially important if you have a commodity product.

Here are a few ideas that will help get potential customers to buy from you:

QR codes or PURLs on a printed direct mailer can drive prospects to a specific landing page on your website where they can quickly purchase your product while they are in a buying mood. Think for a moment about the huge value of what I just said. Before, when interested in your product after receiving one of your promotional pieces, customers had to get in the car and drive to your nearest shop. There may be many hurdles in this process, such as time constraints or prior commitments. How often do you get caught up in the influence of excitement and emotion, and those factors make you want to buy something today that you couldn't be bothered with next week? The power of QR codes is well suited to this situation, because in a matter of seconds a potential buyer can make a purchase before being distracted by something else they need or want to do. When using QR codes, make sure your target audience has smartphones to be able to read them. It is wise to add a PURL just in case they can't read the QR code.

*Good Sports News uses QR codes to make their direct mailer more interactive and offer better incentives for the customer to spend more time with them. While promoting winter sports gear, they sent their target audience a QR code that launches a video. Once the user is online, Good Sports News can continue promoting their products and they can also measure who viewed the video, which may indicate an interest in these products and drive further marketing contact.

*"Case study source: http://www.podi.org/casestudy, a collection of over 500 successful digital and direct marketing solutions in full color."

There are other ideas you can use to make it easy for your customers to buy from you, such as special discounts, as well as an easy buying process for closing sales. Each point in the process in which a customer is confused or unsure about what to do next increases the chance they may go somewhere else to buy.

Tip 12: Successful Marketing Communication Engagement

Example 12: Fabory Germany

Fabory, a German hardware company, offers a great example of capturing attention with a teaser, then telling people what they want to hear by building information about their target. They also made it easy for their target to buy it by providing a relevant incentive.

To direct customers to a new shop they were opening, they first sent a direct mailer in the form of a teaser to intrigue potential customers.

Then they sent out a second mailer with an incentive to go to their website in exchange for a gift. There, they asked potential customers about their product preferences and later used the information to send a more relevant, tailored message.

130   Tip 12: Successful Marketing Communication Engagement

Finally, they followed up with a direct mailer to their targets offering discounts on the products they'd selected as preferences online. They also included a map with the store's location. In this case, response rates were high, at around 20%.

"Case study source: http://www.podi.org/casestudy, a collection of over 500 successful digital and direct marketing solutions in full color."

Tip 13
Don't Forget To Measure and Analyze Your Campaign

You must measure and analyze the success of your campaign against the KPIs that you have already created. By effectively measuring these critical factors, you will know what worked, and what didn't. Then you can analyze why the campaign had the outcome it did, which will help you improve your next campaign.

Measurement

In addition to knowing what you need to measure, it is also important to know when and how to measure as the campaign progresses. You must measure campaigns for two reasons:

1. To know if the campaign was successful or not.

   You need to know how successful the current campaign has been. Has the money, time, and effort spent on the campaign been worth it?

   Typical things to measure in this case are:
   - Response rates
   - Closing rates

- Average purchase size per customer
- Incremental revenue
- Return on marketing investment (ROMI)

2. To analyze the data to improve future campaigns. You need to measure things that will help you understand why and where your campaign was or was not successful.

Critical things to measure are:

- Which profiles responded to which promotional pieces, and which ones didn't respond at all;

- Which profiles bought what, and which ones responded but didn't buy;

- Which profiles were already customers, and which ones weren't.

Measuring techniques for direct mailing campaigns, such as barcodes, QR codes, and URLs/PURLS, can be included on printed mailers. In the past, barcodes were scanned at the place of purchase when a customer bought a product, enabling the marketer to measure how much and what have they sold in a particular campaign. Personalized QR codes and PURLs will take customers to a place of purchase and because they are personalized, not only can we measure responses and bulk sales per product, but most importantly we can measure who responded to what and bought what products and who didn't. This is huge, because it will give us more information when analyzing the data, helping us improve our next campaign. We can also personalize QR codes printed on generic billboards to link to different geographical areas so the marketer could measure which advertising geographies work and which ones didn't. This way, the advertiser can still invest on what is working and tweak what is not to increase their ROMI.

Email campaigns are also very easy to measure and can offer a lot of relevant information. You know who has opened what and when, and who eventually bought something.

Sometimes you need to measure more than you can. In this case, you can use telemarketing after you launch your campaign to test different individuals or companies in your target so you can find out what you want to know.

Analysis

Once the campaign is running and you are collecting data, you must analyze the information to determine the reasons for the outcome. Basically, you will want to know why some things worked in the campaign and why others did not work. In order to do this, you need to know what worked with whom and where it worked, and what didn't. Things to analyze will include:

- Response rates vs. closing rates;
- Why some profiles responded but didn't buy, and why other profiles responded and did buy;
- Why X profiles didn't respond at all;
- Why this campaign was so successful at getting a lot of responses and sales, or why this campaign was such a failure.

Analyzing what happened to whom, when, and where, might help you understand the why, which is critical to improve your next campaign. Ask yourself the following questions to help analyze your campaign.

- Did you hit the right target profiles?
- Did you provide the right message to the right people in the different profiles?
- Why did some messages work in some places with some people, while they didn't with others?
- Did you use the right creative tools to capture attention and/or enhance your message?
- Did you send the message(s) using the right channel(s)?
- Which customers were satisfied, which ones weren't, and why?

It is often easier to make assumptions about why people responded and why they bought than it is to understand why people did not respond and did not buy. However, both are critical to know.

A good analysis is critical and will influence the profiling, messaging, channel, and creativity of future campaigns. It will also help you to improve your product, service and business models.

The more relevant information you have, the more you will learn. We often use telemarketing to promote our products and services and to drive our target to our places of purchase, but we don't often use it to measure our marketing efforts. If you don't have enough information, it is often worth the expense of using telemarketing to get it.

As always, make sure you feed what you learn into your CRM strategy.

"I know half of the money that I invest in advertising is wasted, but I never know which half."
—John Wanamaker

Example 13: Arkansas Democrat-Gazette United States

The campaign was based on four different postcards with varying designs and offers targeting people who had recently canceled their newspaper subscription. Two of the designs addressed Sunday-only subscribers and the other two focused on daily subscribers.

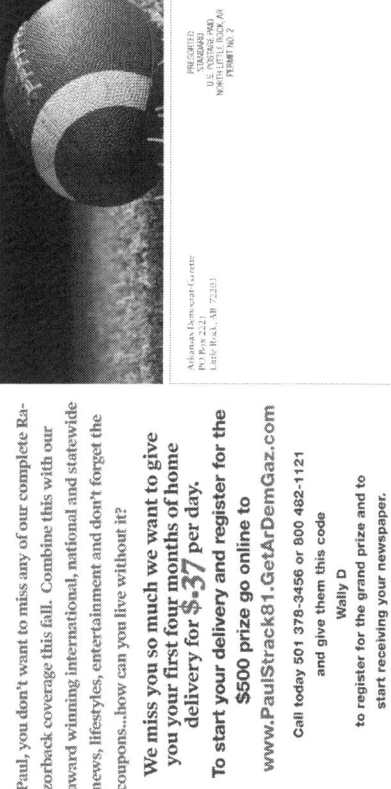

Paul, you don't want to miss any of our complete Razorback coverage this fall. Combine this with our award winning international, national and statewide news, lifestyles, entertainment and don't forget the coupons...how can you live without it?

We miss you so much we want to give you your first four months of home delivery for $.37 per day.

To start your delivery and register for the $500 prize go online to www.PaulStrack81.GetArDemGaz.com

Call today 501 378-3456 or 800 482-1121 and give them this code
Wally D
to register for the grand prize and to start receiving your newspaper.

Arkansas Democrat-Gazette
PO Box 2221
Little Rock, AR 72203

PRESORTED
STANDARD
U.S. POSTAGE PAID
NORTH LITTLE ROCK, AR
PERMIT No. 2

Paul,
Fall football will be here before you know it. Go deep...we've got you covered.

www.PaulStrack81.GetArDemGaz.com

The Digital & Direct Marketing Goose

Sarah, remember those Sunday mornings with your coffee and your newspaper...
all the world's news at your fingertips...complete Razorback sports coverage...local news and events and don't forget the coupons...

We want you back.

Go to www.SarahKirby.GetArDemGaz.com
and register for the $500 prize and get 6 months of Sunday delivery at **HALF PRICE, THAT'S $43.50 FOR THE ENTIRE YEAR!**

or

Call today 501 378-3456 or 800 482-1121
and give them this code

Sunday

to register for the grand prize and t
start receiving your paper next Sunda

Arkansas Democrat Gazette

ARKANSAS' NEWSPAPER

Printed at Little Rock • June 20, 2010   www.SarahKirbyGetArDemGaz.com   82 Pages • 9 Sections

Sarah, You've Been Gone, But We Want You Back...Bad

Go to www.SarahKirby.GetArDemGaz.com to register for $500 prize

Don't miss the fall Razorback and high school football coverage

In the news

■ **Wally Hall**, sports columnist for the Arkansas Democrat-Gazette, believes that reading the Sunday sports section is "like kissing the homecoming queen".

■ **Paul Greenberg**, editorialist for the Arkansas Democrat-Gazette said that living without a quality newspaper is dangerous and intellectually destructive and will almost certainly result

Study Shows Newspapers Inform and Educate Knowledge Improves Life

LITTLE ROCK- University study finds the information

DEMOCRAT GAZETTE PRESS SERVICES

Sarah our records show that you were once a valued subscriber to our newspaper. We are very interested in you becoming a subscriber again and giving you information we are offering great deals, guaranteed prizes and the chance to win $500. As the only statewide newspaper, we cover the state, the country and the world.

help make your money go further. So sign up today and start your Sunday with sports and entertainment with Arkansas's most experienced reporters. Our paper also offers coupons for your fingertips.

138   Tip 13: Don't Forget To Measure and Analyze Your Campaign

The postcards gave recipients two options to respond and take advantage of special pricing—visiting a Personalized URL or calling a toll-free number with a special offer code. These two response vehicles allowed campaign results to be easily tracked. This was an important consideration for the Arkansas Democrat-Gazette since it had been difficult to track results of previous campaigns.

Four different online microsites were designed to fit the art and offer for each postcard version. Upon entering the microsite, visitors could view a short video of Wally Hall, a well-known sports editor and commentator. Visitors were also asked to complete a short survey to register for a free prize drawing. The survey gathered information about visitors' favorite newspaper section and their use of the Classified section. Ninety-nine percent of visitors who completed the online survey renewed their subscription.

Individuals who were interested in renewing their subscription were taken from the microsite to the newspaper's own online subscription pages which were designed to fit the look and feel of the direct mail campaign.

"Case study source: http://www.podi.org/casestudy, a collection of over 500 successful digital and direct marketing solutions in full color."

Tip 14
Use the Right Ingredients

Strategy

Take the time to develop a good plan for your campaign. Follow the methodical process of profiling, populating, engaging, measuring, and analyzing discussed in the previous tips in order to reduce the risks of failure. Again, there are no crystal balls or magic wands in marketing. No one can guarantee response and/or closing rates before they launch a campaign, but when you follow the right methodology and build the right strategy you increase your chances tremendously.

Information and Knowledge

It is easier to sell something to someone you know than to someone you don't—it's as simple as that! Creating customer profiles, as previously discussed, will allow you to know precisely to whom you are selling.

My wife tells me that I am always successfully selling her things and, in a way, she doesn't like it. The reason why I manage to sell her things (ideas, etc.) is because I have good information about her, often using it correctly and always stressing the value to her naturally, without coming off too pushy. This dialogue needs to be at a relationship level and never at a sales level. If she perceives that I am trying to sell her something, I won't be successful. This also applies in business.

There are some general concerns from marketers about data-protection laws. In the past, consumers protected themselves by not sharing their information with marketers and salespeople. Today, because it is easier to gather information surreptitiously, legislation regulates the gathering and usages of customers' and prospects' information. The strategy to deal with either scenario, however, is the same. If you provide value to your target audience that goes far beyond the value of your product, they will often willingly give you permission to use their data, and even expect that you'll do so.

In all my time in sales I never had a customer that was happy with the value that I provided them tell me that I shouldn't know or use information that they in fact provided me. Of course, when I talk to my customers face-to-face I always used information carefully and respectfully.

"Knowing something about your customer is just as important as knowing everything about your product."
—Harvey Mackayokok

*The office of tourism of Bermuda developed a radio commercial about Bermuda that included an incentive for listeners to call a toll-free number. When listeners called, they were asked some relevant questions, and a personalized brochure was mailed out to the caller based on that information. Bermuda tourism has reduced its mailing costs from their original method of sending out generic catalogues that weighed more, and they increased effectiveness, resulting in more visitors coming to Bermuda.

*"Case study source: http://www.podi.org/casestudy, a collection of over 500 successful digital and direct marketing solutions in full color."

Sensitivity

Having the right information is imperative and will greatly increase your chances of getting a better ROMI. Unfortunately, it will not be enough. I have known bad salespeople that were bad not because they did not have relevant information about their target audience, but because they didn't have the sensitivity to use it properly. A good salesperson does not let on what they know about you, and instead uses that information subtly to convince you to buy from them.

The best direct marketers are often the ones that have previous experience selling face-to-face, because they know how to use personalization and understand the importance of using it properly. Basic things like how to call someone will make your message more or less relevant. How should you call someone? Should you call me by my first name or by my last name? Or should you call me Mr. German Sacristan? What if my name was Richard? Do you call me Rich, Rick or Richard? I can tell you that I get tuned off just by the way some people call me, ignoring them completely even if they had something relevant to say to me. Sometimes it is more sensitive not to call someone by name even though you are personalizing. Your decision will be based on the information and relationship that you have with that person, the product or service that you sell, what you are trying to tell them and how, including the channel that you will use to communicate. It is not easy, which is why people with face-to-face selling experience are most likely to make better decisions, not only on how to call people, but also on what to say.

Anything communicated in writing either via print, email, or mobile could be very powerful. Just bear in mind this works both ways so be careful with what you write.

"Words, when they are printed, have a life of their own."
—Carol Burnett

Customization

Customization or personalization has always been the marketer's intention. They've always tried to make their message as relevant and customized as possible to their target audience. When consumers were similar and buying criteria was less diverse, it was easier for them to be relevant to many people with a single message. Today, people are increasingly diverse and buy from you for many different reasons, so in order to tell them what they want to hear you need to adapt your message, creativity, and even the communication channel to fit the person to whom you are talking.

Imagination and Creativity

Creativity is not only related to design, but also to imagination.

"Imagination is more important than knowledge. For knowledge is limited to all we know and understand, while imagination embraces the entire world, and all there will ever be to know and understand."
—Albert Einstein

Being creative and imaginative can help you differentiate and separate your promotional piece from others. It will not only help capture the attention of your target, but may also convince them that they should buy from you. You can have relevant information and great sensitivity, but if you do not have enough imagination and creativity to capture the attention of your target and make your pitch very interesting, you will likely fail.

Time

Campaigns often fail due to the small details. We often rush through the process and strategy or even worse ignore it in order to launch the campaign as quickly as possible. We're obsessed with speed and think that the quicker we launch, the better. However, it is far better to take a little longer and do an outstanding job from a strategic and execution perspective than doing something quick that isn't good enough to capture the attention of your target and convince them that they have to buy from you.

Trust and Interaction

More than ever before, you need the trust of your customer to sell them your products or services. Gathering information from your target audience and using it properly can help you build relationships and, therefore, trust. If you already have that trust, you can use it to further build your profile of information on your target. Either way, you need to continually interact with potential buyers in order to keep information relevant and updated and keep trust intact.

Teasing, Intrigue, Humor, and Fun

All of these, when used correctly, help capture people's attention. They also help you stay in the minds of potential buyers longer. When used properly, these tactics can increase sales through word of mouth, as they create a positive perception about you and what you are selling.

Games

Games can be a compelling interactive tool with which to draw potential buyers closer to you and help you gain word-of-mouth sales. They can also be used to build information about your target. An example could be to add a lottery number on the product that you are promoting. Then encourage potential buyers to go to your place of purchase to find out if they won the prize or not. In the process, you could ask them to subscribe to see if they have won. This way, you not only drive more traffic of potential buyers to your place of purchase, but you build information.

Gifts and Incentives

Free gifts or incentives are powerful tools that encourage buyers to take action. They are often used to close a sale, but can also be used to build the information you need on your target audience. This information will increase your likelihood of making a sale. You can also use that information to better explain the value of what you sell and, in turn, increase sales, customer satisfaction, and loyalty rates.

Clarity

Use clear, simple language to reduce confusion and misunderstanding. If your message is not quickly clear, potential buyers will likely lose interest and go somewhere else.

Recommendations and Testimonials

People rely on recommendations from others like them. People are often unsure about a product until they see someone else buying it or hear of someone else's satisfaction with it. Happy customers are your most powerful and effective sales force.

Consistency and Persistence

Keep a consistent message across all channels, and don't give up! You might need multiple contacts to convince someone to buy from you. Sale cycles are driven by what you sell, where you sell it, and how you sell it. New technologies are an important part of how to sell it and will help you contact more people in a shorter period of time, but they will not reduce the number of visits that you have to execute to make a sale. It will take X number of visits on average for a good salesperson to sell your product face-to-face, so why do you think that you can do it with only one visit? Persistence is everything. If you have sales experience, you probably have had a customer or two that you were just about to give up on. Then you decided to give it one more shot, and that's when you made the sale. It is very important not to give up on the right customers and prospects, but you also must be careful not to waste time with the wrong ones.

COMgraph, in Poland, needed to communicate to their target audience more than once in order to generate the desired action. To do so, they sent out one piece of this puzzle every four days. On the front of each piece was a part of the larger puzzle image, while on the back each time was a new reason for their target to act. You often must reach out to your audience more than once, and this was a creative way of doing so.

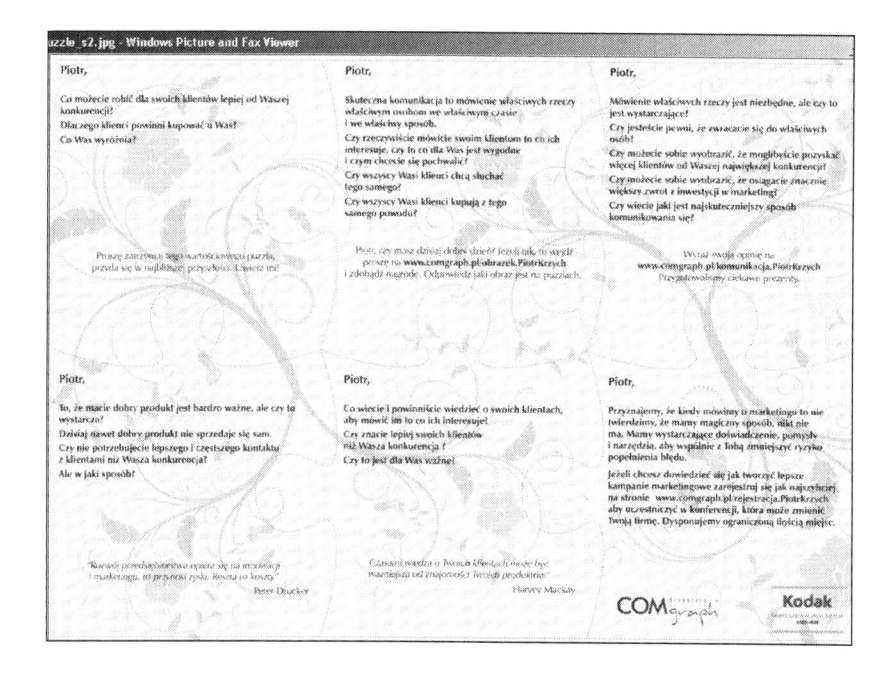

Proper Channels

Use the channels your customers prefer and the ones that fit your strategy best, not just the ones that are the easiest or have the lowest cost. Something that costs less can, in the end, be more expensive if it fails to do what it was supposed to. Cheap or expensive is not measured by the cost but by the ROMI. As we discussed earlier, don't begin your strategy with the channel, or you will limit yourself and increase the risks of failure. The channel is part of the strategy, not the strategy itself. Look past the excitement of the new media channels and stick to your strategy, even if that means using some of the tried-and-true channels such as postal mail, telemarketing, etc., as they all have their place. You need to know where you are going and what are you carrying in order to choose the right channel.

In the end, the best channel to communicate through is not the Internet, TV, or radio; it is word of mouth, because then you're using people with better information and relationships than you have to sell your products.

Testing

Why aren't you checking with the expert before you launch a campaign? As a marketer, you are not the expert, the consumer is. The consumer tells us if we are right or wrong. Digital technologies allow you to constantly and inexpensively test with some experts (buyers) before you actually commit to your big campaign. You can test your campaign with a small representation of your target audience to learn how they react to it. Then apply the proper adjustments before you launch your big campaign. This exercise will reduce your risk of failure.

Money

It is not free to capture the attention of your target, nor is it free to be relevant. The key is not only knowing how much money to invest, but also how to invest it. Remember, it isn't about trying to contact everyone, but rather trying to contact the right ones. It is about investing your marketing money with the right potential buyers and the ones you can afford to contact.

Often, we don't have enough marketing budget to contact everyone we'd like to. In those cases, it's more effective to correctly contact a few than incorrectly contact everyone. The key is determining how much you have to invest per potential buyer while still having a real chance at selling them. Divide your marketing budget by that number, and you will get the number of potential buyers that you can afford to contact at this particular time.

Marketing and Sales Integration

Marketing will make salespeople more productive and vice versa, but, unfortunately, marketing and salespeople often do not work closely enough together. Companies with marketing and sales reps and big enough budgets often invest in a CRM system in order to have a common working platform.

Both sales and marketing should feed information into the system to increase sales productivity. If salespeople don't feed information into the CRM system, marketing will not have the opportunity to create better, more effective campaigns that could generate more leads. Many salespeople don't see enough value in the CRM system to sacrifice selling time in order to feed information into it. A proper in-house education and incentive program should be put in place to increase usage because all will benefit in the end.

Measuring and Analysis

After a marketing campaign, make sure you know what happened, why it happened, and how it happened so you will have a chance to do better next time. Measurement and analysis will increase your chances of success on your next campaign.

Fearlessness and Courage

"What would you attempt to do if you knew you could not fail?"
—Dr. Robert Schuller

Your strategy will not likely be perfect the first time so don't give up. Fear can cause you to give up and can also stop you from taking chances and doing the right things. The methodical campaign process discussed in this book will guide you in making the right decisions, while also showing you the potential ROMI on those decisions, which will, in the end, help your overcome the fear.

Partners

You will likely not have all the ingredients to make a successful campaign yourself, so make sure you find the right partners that can help you. As marketers, we never know everything we need to know, as there is a holistic aspect of marketing related to the imagination and sensitivity that goes beyond knowledge. The interaction with partners should never become a competition about knowledge. Find the right partners that make the campaign team more experienced, functional, and effective. My best campaigns have always involved collaboration with other people. It is all about teamwork, and the right people can create the right chemistry that makes the team better. You can create something as a team that could not have been created with just one person. This video reinforces partnerships.

http://www.youtube.com/watch?v=eNwMut3-z1Y&feature=relmfu, uploaded by TheCognitiveMedia on Sep 21, 2010, Steven Johnson —Where Good Ideas Come From

My father taught me the best lesson about building a strong partnership with a critical supplier. His current business is about selling promotional items to brands. All these items have to be screen-printed with a brand logo, customer contact information, and sometimes even a marketing pitch. My father has partnered with best screen printer in Spain to do that job. The problem is that his competitors also use the same supplier. Quality and turnaround are critical for so my father pays more to the screen printer when he can afford to without the screen printer asking him to do so. Think about this for a second. You are the screen printer and give your quote to a customer. Then the customer asks you to increase the price 20%. I have seen that screen printer working day and night for my father doing whatever it takes to get the job done. This is what a real partnership is all about—helping each other.

"It is amazing what you can accomplish if you don't care who gets the credit."
—Harry S. Truman

Summary

All these ingredients are imperative to reduce the risks of failure, but one of the most critical things when working with direct marketing is to understand that you are copying a salesperson. The majority of campaigns that fail do so because they forget that. If you wouldn't say something to your prospects face-to-face, why would you put it in print or email? If in face-to-face sales you need to talk with your prospects a certain number of times, why would that number change if when you use marketing tools such as email or post? Always remember that most concepts that apply to your salespeople will likely apply to your marketing efforts. So before you start a campaign, you should ask yourself how you would sell your product face-to-face and apply similar fundamentals.

"Advertising is what you do when you can't be there face to face."
—Fairfax Cone

Example 14: One-to-One Mexico

A creative agency in Mexico called One to One together with Kodak planned a direct marketing campaign in Mexico City to invite marketers to a seminar. The marketing seminar was about sharing relevant ideas and strategies that could help a marketer improve their ROMI.

First a teaser mailer was sent out. The mailer opened up into a cardboard picture frame with some relevant messages on it. The tone of the campaign was around picture frames as there was an incentive to win a digital picture frame. Some recipients utilized the cardboard frame to display some family photos at their working desk.

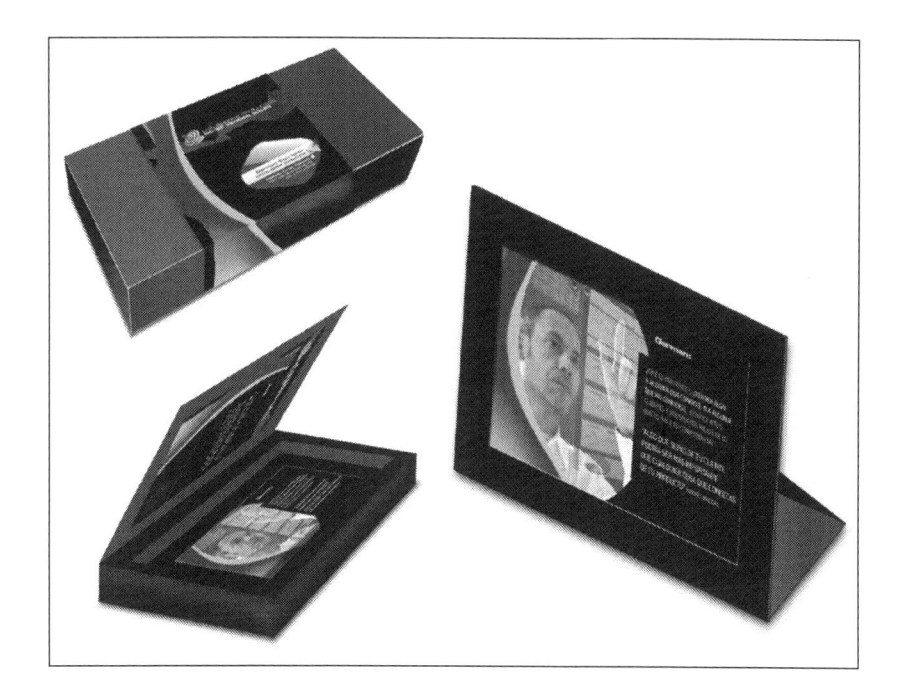

A second mailer was sent out simulating the control remote of the digital picture frame that they could win. Some relevant messages were also displayed on the control remote.

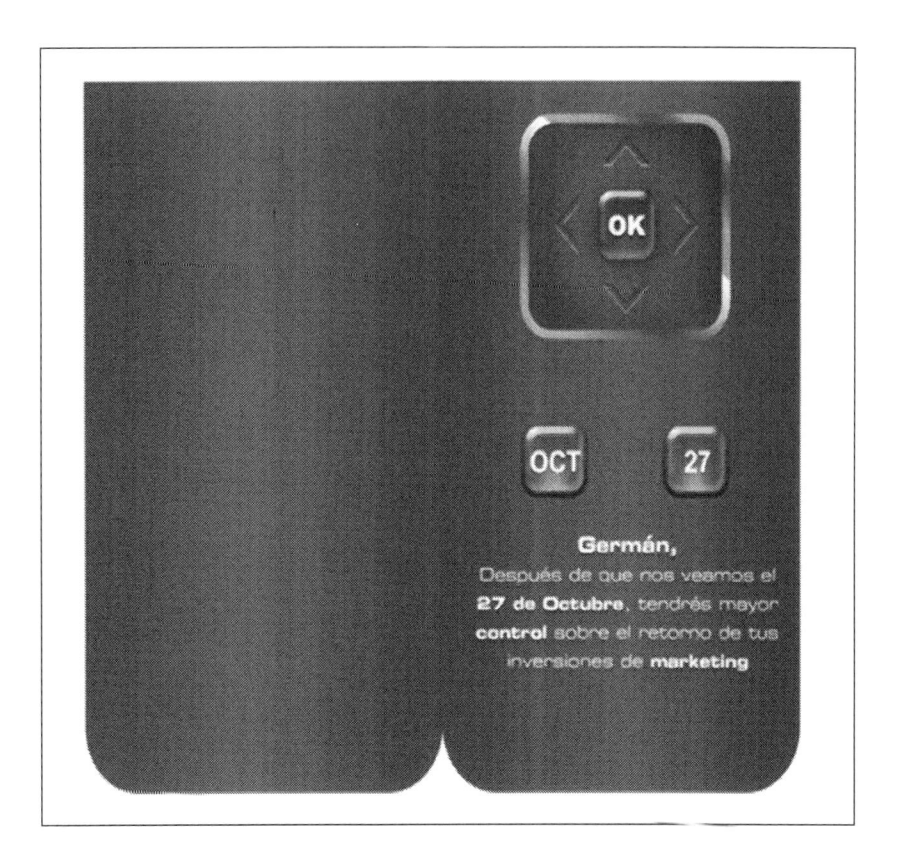

The third mailer was sent out as an empty box simulating the box of the digital picture frame that they could win. In addition, relevant messages were shown, including a URL to send recipients to a registration page where they could learn more about the seminar as well as to register.

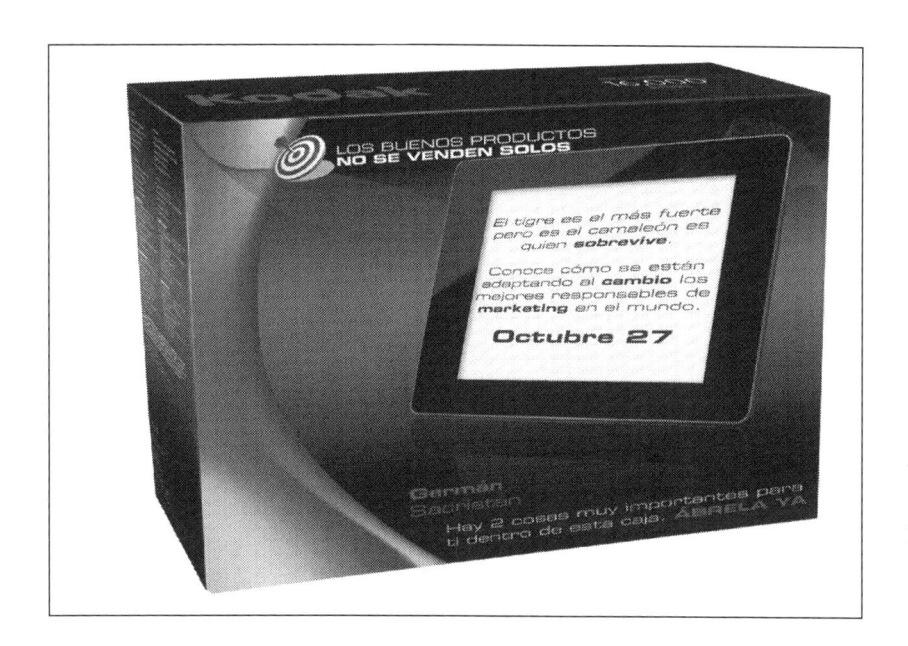

After that, an email campaign of two touches was sent out followed by telemarketing. The campaign delivered 21% response rate. Furthermore, at the end of the seminar One to One delivered a personal envelope message to all the attendees while still there. A plastic butterfly flew up in the air when attendees opened their envelopes. How about that for great creativity!

STEVE,
La trascendencia de
tu marca
está en tus manos...
Nosotros te damos el impulso.
¡Elévate!
ONE TO ONE
STEVE

Tip

15 Beware of the Ten Reasons Campaigns Fail

1. Lack of, or incorrect strategy and focus

   - Failure to properly examine and analyze your own product/company, market and history, or focusing too much on your desire to sell and not enough on satisfying your targets needs.

2. Talking to the wrong people or failing to reach the right target audience

   - Lack of understanding of who buys from you.
   - Poor data, lack of relevant information.
   - Failure to measure and analyze previous campaigns.
   - Speculating or guessing, rather than relying on data.
   - Picking the wrong channel to reach your target audience.

3. Lack of information, imagination and sensitivity

   - Lack of a strategy to collect information.

- Lack of a tool to keep and organize information.
- Lack of imagination, design experience and creativity.
- Lack of copywriting experience and common sense, poorly written copy.

4. Wrong channel
   - Building the campaign around the channel rather than making the channel part of the campaign.
5. Forgetting to check with the expert
   - Check with the consumer before you launch the campaign.
6. You gave up too soon
   - How many times do you have to contact a prospect to make them buy from you? Do not give up before then!

"If you want the rainbow you gotta put up with the rain."
—**Dolly Parton**

7. You didn't make it easy for prospects to buy from you so they went somewhere else.
8. Incorrect use of the marketing budget
   - Are you spending enough per prospect/customer to turn them around?
   - Are you trying to talk to too many people without having the budget to do so?
9. You didn't pay enough attention to detail and/or rushed through the campaign. Follow a good methodology, and pay careful attention to each step.
10. You failed to copy an effective salesperson

"Success is how high you bounce when you hit the bottom."
—**General George Patton**

Example 15: Orthodontics United States

Here is an example of someone having the proper information but using it incorrectly.

I visited a dentist with my son Matthew twice. My son, who is only nine years old, received a mailer saying: "Dear Matthew, You've seen improvements in your children's appearance, self-esteem, and confidence; now it's your turn, Mom and Dad!. My son obviously does not have children; the fact that the dentist's marketing team didn't properly use what they knew about my son is reinforced with the message "Now it's your turn, Mom and Dad!"

The dentist has enough information about my son to know he is not old enough to be married or have kids. When you make a mistake like the one here, personalization can amplify a negative impression. It isn't good enough to have relevant data—you also need to use it properly. On the other hand, personalization can work very well when used properly.

Even if the dentist got it right by addressing me as the father of my son, he also knew that two of our visits to his office were for consultation, so why would I see improvement on my son's self-esteem?

Tip 16
Become a Marketing God

- Urgency does not stop the best marketers from doing something important every day/week.
- They welcome and embrace change.

"The tiger is the mightiest, but the chameleon is the one who's going to endure!"
—Buddha

- They talk very little about their products and a lot about how they can help their customers. They are very passionate and excited about helping their customers.
- They tell their customers what they want to hear rather than what they want to say.
- They know their customers better than their competitors do.
- They recognize that they are not the experts.
- They always start with the right methodology that helps them build the right strategy.
- They enlist relevant partners who make their pitch/product stronger.

- They pay close attention to and build the correct market perception.
- They market internally.
- They pay great attention to detail, either on their own or through delegation.
- They do the simple things better than their competitors.
- They have great imagination and sensitivity.
- They constantly measure and analyze their activities.
- They are executers!

"Well done is better than well said."
—Benjamin Franklin

- They never, ever GIVE UP!

"Courage is the ability to go from failure to failure without loss of enthusiasm."
—Winston Churchill

Example 16: Chick-fil-A United States

Chick-fil-A wanted two things: establish a customer database and increase store traffic.

A plastic postcard with two perforated cards, featuring campaign offers, was mailed to consumers in the Covington, Louisiana area. Recipients were instructed to log on to their Personalized URL in order to activate their two offers, and go into the store to redeem them.

In addition to the direct mail postcards, cards were also given to local businesses such as Walmart and Target, where the cards were given out to employees. These cards directed recipients to visit a generic URL tied to the campaign. Upon visiting either the Personalized URL or generic URL, users were taken to a customized microsite for the Chick-fil-A campaign.

Users validated their contact information on the first screen, selected the offer they wanted to activate, and answered a few questions from Chick-fil-A. Next, users were given the opportunity to share the offer on up to 265 social networks, email, and SMS. All recipients who shared the offer with friends were entered into a sweepstakes.

Chick-fil-A customers' primary sharing outlet was Facebook, with 1,218 users posting the offer in their newsfeed. This brought in an additional 6,499 users to the site. Twitter fans proved very responsive to the offer, with 115 users tweeting the offer and 1,185 users responding and coming into the microsite through a tweet, almost a 1-to-10 response. Users also opted to share the offer through email and SMS.

After completing the process, users were able to print the offer (if they had not received the offer in the mail) and bring it into the store for redemption.

"Case study source: http://www.podi.org/casestudy, a collection of over 500 successful digital and direct marketing solutions in full color."

Appendix A

Free-Bee Example: UNICEF Brazil and Final Thought!

The database was composed of donor records that included data on the value and reasons for the recipient's last donation. The list was segmented into three groups—a control group and two groups that would receive personalized packages. The theme of the personalized package, either education or health, was based on the donor's reason for their last contribution. All of the personalized communication pieces, direct mail with a personalized letter, email, PURLs and personalized landing pages, incorporated one-to-one marketing and customized offerings.

Recipients were encouraged to go to their PURL and visit their personalized donation page. They could also complete a survey and refer friends as potential donors. The response channels were return mail postcards or the PURL.

Significant Results Reported by User:

Total responses in terms of monthly donations:

- The response rate for the healthcare package was 232% more than the control.

- The response rate for the education package was 106% more than the control.

Total donations at 12 months:

- The healthcare package generated 111% more funds than the control.
- The education package generated 48% more funds than the control.

Return on Investment (ROI):

- The ROI for the healthcare package was 41% greater than the control.
- The education donations were equal to the control at 12 months, but raised 48% more for every year that the donors remained active.

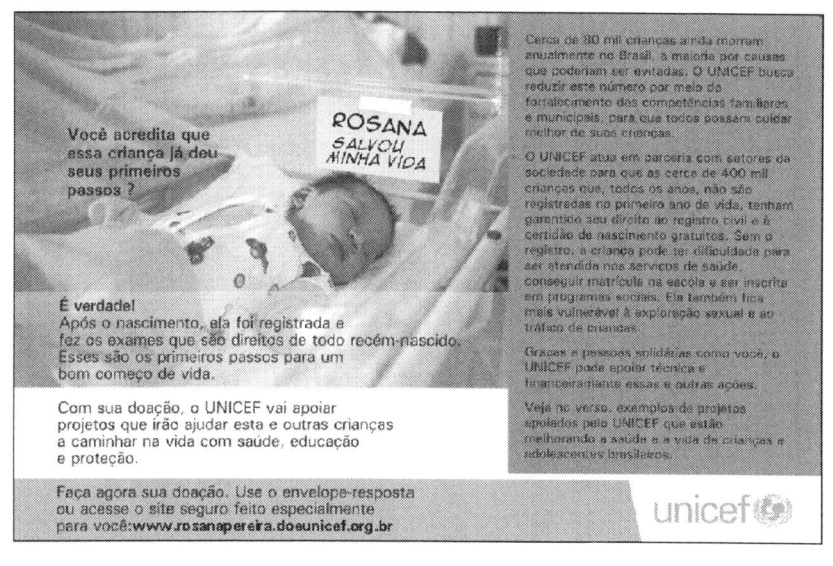

"Case study source: http://www.podi.org/casestudy, a collection of over 500 successful digital and direct marketing solutions in full color."

The Digital & Direct Marketing Goose 169

Final Thought!

Big brands and their marketers have been impatiently waiting for the arrival of the new marketing goose that will make up for the decline in golden eggs since the height of television advertising. In the past, almost anything advertised delivered a mass production of golden eggs. Today, the market is much different, and the new media, although extremely strong and relevant, can't solve the problem if it's not used properly. Now, more than ever, we need to go back to the basics to build better strategies. The methodology and ingredients discussed in this book will help you do just that!

Author

About the Author

German Sacristan offers a wealth of international sales, marketing, and business development experience. His proven ability to grow market share from 26% to 80% has lead to successfully launching direct marketing campaigns and achieving double-digit response rates in the process. He is highly passionate about sales and marketing, and developed them naturally at an early age while doing TV commercials and helping customers at his family's businesses. He values the basics and fundamentals of face-to-face marketing and enjoys using the new technologies and channels to apply those fundamentals in today's marketplace.

You can contact German at: marketinggoose@gmail.com and http://www.marketinggoose.com.

Books

Other Happy About® Books

Purchase these books at Happy About http://happyabout.com or at other online and physical bookstores.

42 Rules of Marketing

The reader will be reminded of what they know they should be doing, but don't do. They will find useful ideas and insights that help them improve the quality of their marketing efforts.

Paperback: $19.95
eBook: $14.95

Red Fire Branding

Liz Goodgold directs her works towards the business-to-business market to help small business owners, entrepreneurs, sales professionals, or anyone who is looking to create an indelible image.

Hardcover: $39.95
Paperback: $19.95
eBook: $14.95

Ignite!

In this how-to business book, Sal, a veteran of corporate potential maximization, shows the path to igniting the potential of new leaders.

Paperback: $19.95
eBook: $14.95

#MANAGING YOUR VIRTUAL BOSS tweet Book01

You will learn to understand, and even empathize, with the secret fears your boss has in managing you, and master practical strategies you can use to ensure your success.

Paperback: $19.95
eBook: $14.95

Made in the USA
Charleston, SC
02 February 2013